ALSO BY MAIDA HEATTER

Maida Heatter's Book of Great Desserts (1974)
Maida Heatter's Book of Great Cookies (1977)
Maida Heatter's Book of Great Chocolate Desserts (1980)
Maida Heatter's New Book of Great Desserts (1982)
Maida Heatter's Book of Great American Desserts (1985)
Maida Heatter's Greatest Dessert Book Ever (1990)

MAIDA HEATTER'S BRAND-NEW BOOK OF GREAT COOKIES

Maida Heatter's Brand-New Book of Great Cookies

Illustrations by the author

RANDOM HOUSE
NEW YORK

Library of Congress Cataloging-in-Publication Data

Heatter, Maida.
Maida Heatter's brand-new book of great cookies / Maida Heatter.
p.   cm.
Includes index.
ISBN 0-679-43874-2
1. Cookies.   I. Title.
TX772.H398   1995
641.8´654—dc20   95-5250

Manufactured in the United States of America
on acid-free paper

2 4 6 8 9 7 5 3

Book design by Carole Lowenstein

Contents

Happiness Is Baking Cookies

Often, when I'm introduced to someone new, I am asked if I bake all these cookies myself. Yes, I do. I do—I do—I do. (And usually it is many more times than that.) And then, "What do you do with all the cookies?" I've had a few problems in my life, but what to do with cookies has never been one of them. The answer is that I give them away. And it is magic. It is the original "How to Win Friends." (It is called cookie diplomacy.) It makes people happy and that, in turn, makes me happy. Happiness is baking cookies. Happiness is giving them away. And serving them, and eating them, talking about them, reading and writing about them, thinking about them, and sharing them with you.

I love it all, and I love it more all the time. Every time I bake cookies (even the ones I make over and over again), it's always exciting.

I wish you happy cookies—and much cookie happiness.

Maida Heatter
Miami Beach, Florida
1995

In
the
Kitchen

BAKING PAN LINER PAPER, A.K.A. BAKING PARCHMENT

This is paper that is coated on both sides with silicone, which prevents cookies from sticking. It also controls the cookies' shapes (if you butter the cookie sheets, the cookies might run out and be too thin on the edges). These are the reasons I use it. But also, I don't object to the fact that I hardly ever have to wash a cookie sheet. And if I have too many sheets of cookies, I prepare the cookies all at once on pieces of baking pan liner paper, and then just slide a cookie sheet under the paper, and it's OK if the sheet is still hot.

In many or most of these recipes the directions say to line the sheets with baking pan liner paper or aluminum foil. Aluminum foil usually does almost the same thing that the paper does.

The baking pan liner paper comes on a roll like wax paper and is generally available in kitchen shops and hardware stores. It also comes in very large sheets in a big box available at wholesale paper companies and wholesale bakery supply stores. I bought a box about ten years ago and I just recently used the last sheet and had to buy another box. Unless you have a bakery, or unless you write cookie books, a box might be more than you want. But it's such great stuff, it's worth trying to find someone (or some two or three or more) to share it with.

The large sheets are twice as large as most cookie sheets. I work with ten or twenty pieces of it. I fold them in half, and then with a large, heavy, sharp knife, cut through the fold. I then have enough for several days of baking.

If you do a lot of cookie baking, try to get the large box. You'll love it.

CLEAR CELLOPHANE

I wrap most of the cookies I make in clear cellophane. If the cookies are like brownies, I wrap them individually, but if the cookies are large, round cookies, I wrap them two together, bottoms together.

I love doing it—I mean, it's fun. But quite aside from that, it protects the cookies. It keeps them fresh, and in many cases it prevents crumbling. Certainly, if you want to give (or mail) some cookies, it is so easy and so nice if they are individually wrapped.

I use clear cellophane; wax paper or aluminum foil would work as well, but not plastic wrap. (I use plastic wrap a lot, but it is just not practical for wrapping cookies individually.)

Clear cellophane might be difficult to find (it is for me). Now I buy it from the Party Bazaar featuring Dennison's products in Yonkers, New York. (Phone 914-965-1465.) It comes in a box with a cutter edge, and is twenty inches wide and one hundred feet long.

I cut off a long piece (maybe about three yards), fold it in half, cut through the fold with a long, sharp knife, fold again, cut again, then fold through the width and cut it until it is the size I want (that depends on the size of the cookies).

When the cellophane is cut—and the cookies are ready—lay out as many pieces of cut cellophane as you will need (or as many as you have room for). Place a cookie in the center of each piece of cellophane (1). Bring the two ends ends together up over the top (2). Fold over twice so that the second fold brings the cellophane tight against the cookie (3, 4). Now, fold in the corners of each end, making a triangular point (5), and then fold the triangle down under the cookie (6). See opposite.

COOKIE CUTTERS

Obviously it is not necessary to use exactly the same size or shape cutter that the recipe mentions; this is just a guide. Cutters should be sharp, with no rough edges. If the cutter sticks to the dough, dip it in flour each time you use it.

Always start cutting at the edge of the rolled-out dough and work toward the center, cutting the cookies as close to each other as possible.

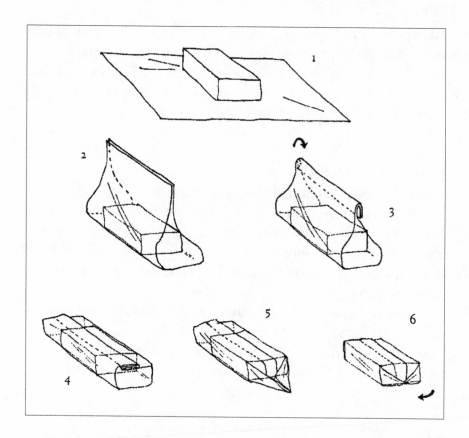

COOKIE JARS

Cookie jars should be airtight. Many of the charming and artistic colorful ones I have seen are not. Glass jars with ground glass around the rim and the cover are airtight. Some plastic or glass jars with a rubber ring around the top are also airtight. But if I have a choice, I use Rubbermaid containers—these are airtight for sure.

CRYSTAL SUGAR

A few of these recipes call for crystal sugar. It is more coarse than granulated sugar, and is very attractive on certain cookies. It can be bought from Sweet Celebrations (formerly Maid of Scandinavia) in Minneapolis, Minnesota (800-480-2505). It comes in 1-pound bags and is labeled "Medium Grain."

There is another sugar, in pieces the same size as crystal sugar, labeled "Vanilla Sugar, Turbinado style." It has a beautiful golden color, and a delicious vanilla-bean flavor. It comes in 3- to 7-ounce jars with a piece of fresh vanilla bean in each jar. The company that makes it is India Tree in Seattle, Washington. (800-270-0293. Tell them you got their number from me.)

DOUBLE BOILER

A double boiler is important, most especially for melting chocolate, which should never come in close contact with high heat or it will burn. For melting chocolate with no other ingredients, make absolutely, positively sure that the top of the double boiler is bone dry. Just a drop of water would spoil the chocolate (as in dry, lumpy, unmanageable).

If necessary, you can create a double boiler by placing the ingredient(s) in a heat-proof bowl over a pot containing an inch or so of hot water. The bowl should be wide enough so that the rim of the bowl rests on the rim of the pot and the bowl is supported above the water.

DRIED PITTED SOUR CHERRIES

I love them in cookies and use them often. Usually, when a recipe calls for raisins, I use a mixture of sour cherries and raisins. Sometimes I use all cherries in place of raisins. A few specialty food stores sell them, but I buy them from American Spoon Foods in Petoskey, Michigan (800-222-5886). Ask for their gorgeous catalog.

FLOUR SIFTER

While I was working on one of these recipes, I made it over and over and over again. A little more of something, a little less of something else. Bake it longer. Bake it less. Et cetera. I was finally satisfied, and everyone raved about the cookies. So I typed the recipe and went on to other things.

Time passed, and then one day I made the cookies again. The recipe didn't work. I knew the recipe was right, so I guessed I had just made some silly little mistake. I made them again, and again, carefully following the recipe—and it still didn't work.

For a while I thought that was it. I was finished. I would never bake another cookie. But I soon found out what had gone wrong. I was using unsifted flour instead of sifted flour.

The reason I am telling you this long, sad story is to point out the importance of reading every word of a recipe—and to point out how important it is to sift the flour before you measure it, if that is what the recipe calls for. Even if the bag says it is sifted, you must sift it just before measuring in order to use the same amount that I used. When it stands, it packs down. And that can make a big difference in a recipe.

I use a triple sifter, but I suspect that any sifter, single, double, or triple—or even a strainer—will be OK. You are only sifting it to aerate it.

Sift the flour onto a large piece of paper. Make sure that there is no flour left in the sifter.

If the flour is to be sifted with other dry ingredients, transfer the sifter to another piece of paper. Measure the sifted flour, place it in the sifter, add the other dry ingredients, and sift again. And again, make sure that there is nothing left in the sifter.

GRATER

To make grated lemon or orange rind I use a four-sided metal grater. Each side has different size and shape openings. I use the side with small round openings, definitely not the side with diamond-shaped openings. The rind never sticks, and I don't have any trouble with it.

Place a piece of wax paper or baking parchment on your work surface and place the grater on the paper. I've seen people hold the grater in the air over a mixing bowl. Wrong. You must be able to press firmly on the grater; to do this, the grater must be resting on a secure surface.

The important thing when using this kind of grater is not to grate your fingers. Hold the fruit firmly, and be conscious of your fingers. They should not be too close to the grater.

The fruit should be cold and firm (when it is soft, it doesn't want to be grated). Grate just a few times up and down over one part of the fruit, and then turn the fruit to the next area. Don't get any more of the white than you have to; what you want is the colored part.

MEASURING CUPS

A beautiful young lady friend of mine told me that she had trouble with a certain cookie recipe from one of my books. I invited her into the kitchen for a demonstration. The first thing I did was to take out the flour sifter and the set of metal measuring cups. She said, "I don't have those—the cups." I asked her how she had measured the 1⅓ cups of flour the recipe called for. She looked around the kitchen, and when she saw the 4-cup Pyrex measuring cup, she pointed to it and matter-of-factly said that that was what she had used.

That was the end—or the beginning—of the demonstration. We found out that she had done everything else right. But you cannot measure 1⅓ cups of flour in a glass measuring cup. Those cups are made for measuring liquids. You must have a set of graded metal cups made for measuring dry ingredients. Fill the cup to overflowing, and then cut off the excess with a metal spatula or any straight edge.

When you measure liquids, the glass cup should be at eye level and you should pour into it until the liquid reaches the correct line for the amount you want.

MEASURING SPOONS

Standard measuring spoons must be used for correct measurements. They come in sets of four: ¼ teaspoon, ½ teaspoon, 1 teaspoon, and 1 tablespoon. When measuring dry ingredients, fill the spoon to overflowing and then scrape off the excess with a small metal spatula or the flat side of a knife.

NUTS

To skin hazelnuts, spread them on a jelly roll pan and bake at 350 degrees for 15 to 20 minutes, or until the skins parch and begin to flake off. Then wrap them in a towel and let them stand for 15 to 20 minutes. Then, working with a small amount of the nuts at a time, place them on a large, coarse towel (I use a terry cloth bath towel). Fold part of the towel over to enclose the nuts. Rub firmly against the towel, or hold that part of the towel between both hands and rub back and forth. The handling and the texture of the towel will cause most of the skins to flake off. Pick out the nuts and discard the skins. Don't worry about the few little pieces of skin that may remain.

If you can possibly buy them blanched (they are available) do it. Skinning these is slow and tedious.

It is easier to skin almonds—just cover them with boiling water. The skin will loosen almost immediately. Spoon out a few nuts at a time and, one by one, hold them under cold running water and squeeze them between your thumb and forefinger. The nuts will pop out and the skins will remain. Place the peeled almonds on a towel to dry. Then spread them in a shallow pan and put them in a preheated 200-degree oven for about 30 minutes, or until completely dry.

Always store nuts in the freezer or refrigerator.

OVEN THERMOMETER

A fine professional chef friend of mine came to visit me. He told me that he had recently taught a cooking class for a large group of people.

The first thing he demonstrated was the dessert, ice cream and cookies. While the ice cream was churning, he made the cookies. He was very familiar with the recipe. They were supposed to bake for ten to twelve minutes. After ten minutes he checked the cookies and they were still soft and runny. A few minutes later they were almost the same. I don't know how long it took for them to bake, but they never did get the nice golden color or the crisp texture he had promised.

After the class was over he got an oven thermometer, tested the oven temperature, and found that it was 100 degrees too low.

I said, "Next time, test the oven *before* you bake, not after."

It can make or break the recipe.

Hardware stores and kitchen shops sell the Taylor oven thermometer, which is not expensive and is very dependable.

Place the thermometer in the middle of the oven and preheat the oven at least twenty minutes ahead of time. If the temperature is too high or too low, adjust the thermostat until the thermometer registers the temperature you want.

Do this even if (maybe especially if) you have a brand-new oven.

PASTRY BAG

A few of these cookies are shaped with a pastry bag. The best bags are made of soft canvas and are coated only on the inside with plastic. The small opening in the pointed end of the bag generally has to be cut a bit larger to make room for a metal tube (tip) to fit into the bag.

It is easier to work with a bag that is too large than one that is too small—use a large bag.

After using, the bag should be washed in hot soapy water, rinsed well, and hung up to dry. Or you can just place it upright over a glass or a jar to dry.

PASTRY BRUSH

Use a good one or the bristles will come out while you are using it. Kitchen shops sell them, but I sometimes use a good-quality artist's watercolor brush in a large size. It is softer and does a very good job.

Each time, after using it, rub it gently onto a cake of soap until very foamy, then rinse well.

PASTRY CLOTH

I can't imagine making rolled-out cookies without a pastry cloth because it prevents the dough from sticking. Buy the largest and heaviest cloth you can find. With your hands, rub flour firmly into the cloth. Then rub in some more, until you can't rub in any more. While you are rolling out the dough it will probably be necessary to reflour the cloth a few times. You can move the dough to one side, or just sprinkle some flour under the dough, but don't add any more flour than you need.

A rolling-pin cover usually comes with a pastry cloth. I am not in the habit of using one, but you might like it. However, flour your rolling pin, covered or not, and reflour it as necessary.

Although some pastry cloths come with literature that says they are coated with something and should not be washed, any time it looks like the cloth might have absorbed some butter from the dough, I wash it, dry it, and iron it.

REVERSING COOKIE SHEETS IN THE OVEN

Every oven I know of registers different temperatures in different parts of the oven. I have two Thermador ovens and they are hotter in the back than in the front. Therefore, many of these recipes say to bake two sheets at a time and to reverse the sheets top to bottom and front to back during baking to insure even browning. Or the instructions are to bake one sheet at a time and reverse the sheet front to back during baking.

I'm good at it. I can bake a whole batch of cookies and have them all come out exactly the same color. So can you. Reversing the pans is what does it.

But when you open the oven door to do the reversing, do it as quickly as you can in order not to let the oven cool off too much.

ROLLING PINS

I have a large collection of rolling pins in all sizes and all shapes. The pin that is tapered at both ends—I believe it is called a French-type rolling pin—is generally used when making a circle, as for a pie. The straight pin—the heavier the better—is used for rolling a square or oblong, as you would want for cookies to be cut out with cookie cutters.

RUBBER SPATULAS

Rubber spatulas (rubber is better than plastic) are indispensable. They are necessary for scraping the bowl of an electric mixer while adding ingredients in order to keep everything well mixed. And for scraping all the dough out of the bowl. And for folding, stirring, mixing, et cetera. They are made in three sizes, but medium is the one you will have the most use for. You might not use the large one often, but when you want it, you'll be mighty glad if you have it.

RULER

On my kitchen counter, in the jar that holds rubber and wooden spatulas, metal spatulas, pastry brushes, ladles, and large spoons, there is also a long ruler. It is an essential kitchen tool, most especially for cookies. Use it to measure the thickness of rolled-out dough, and the thickness of icebox cookie slices (place the ruler on top of the bar or roll of chilled dough, make small scoring marks with the tip of a small, sharp knife, then remove the ruler and cut the slices). Use the ruler to measure the diameter of cookie cutters, the size of cake pans, and most especially use it for marking bar cookies (like brownies) in order to cut them the same size (measure with the ruler and mark by inserting toothpicks).

TIMING

Recently I received a letter from a woman who had made a cookie recipe of mine. The recipe said to bake for a certain number of minutes. When the time was up, she opened the oven door and saw that the cookies were burned. All the ingredients, and the time she spent, were wasted.

Always, in baking, timing can only be a rough guide. You must check before the time is up. You must be prepared for cookies to bake either more or less time than a recipe calls for. Ovens vary. Do not walk away or answer the phone or do anything else when you have cookies in the oven. Watch them. Check on them. Test them. Don't let them burn.

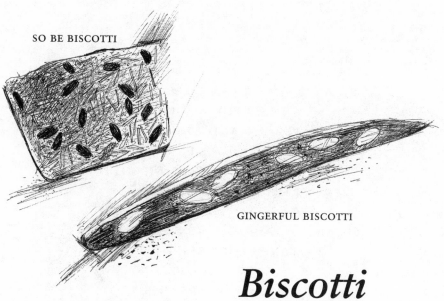

SO BE BISCOTTI

GINGERFUL BISCOTTI

Biscotti
and
Zwieback

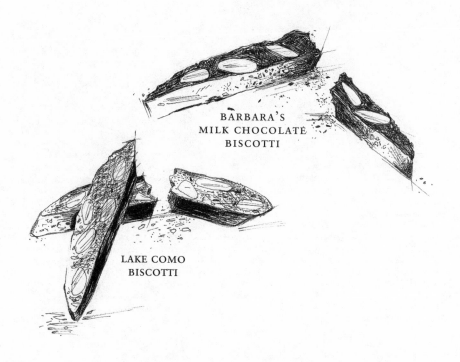

BARBARA'S
MILK CHOCOLATE
BISCOTTI

LAKE COMO
BISCOTTI

BISCOTTI

"Biscotti! Biscotti! Biscotti! That's all I see and smell and hear about all over the house all day and all night. I am sick and tired of biscotti. I would give anything for a brownie or a bran muffin or a slice of pound cake. But no! You're driving me nuts with your ——— biscotti. ——— you and your ——— biscotti."

The above declaration was repeated to me by Hope Fuller, a neighbor and friend whose cousin had come to a cooking class I gave. Biscotti was one of the recipes I taught. The cousin, a young married man, went home and started to bake biscotti, and he couldn't stop. His wife (who doesn't bake) was fed up. I understand the young man well. I can't stop either. But no one complains to me about it. They wouldn't dare!

Biscotti, in Italian, means "cookies." It also means "bake twice." In any event, most of us think of one particular cookie when we hear the word. A long, narrow cookie, dry, crisp, crunchy, and hard. It is baked twice, once in an oval free-form loaf shape or in a loaf pan, and then again after the loaf is cut into slices or into narrow finger-shaped cookies somewhat like zwieback (which means "twice-baked" in German). They have been making varieties of biscotti in Italy since the thirteenth century, and biscotti have recently become wildly popular in America. There is a whole cookbook of just biscotti recipes. Many pasta/pizza shops, chic kitchen shops, gourmet food stores, and Italian restaurants have a tall glass jar of biscotti on display, and they sell like hotcakes. Packaged biscotti, with attractive labels, sell for as much as seven to ten dollars (or more) for a 6- or 7-ounce package. (And they are not as good as these.)

Craig Claiborne says that these make his pulse quicken and that he finds it difficult to limit himself to only two or three or even four. He can't resist them. Wolfgang Puck often serves biscotti in his famous California restaurants along with whatever dessert a customer has ordered.

Italians often serve biscotti for breakfast with espresso or coffee, or after a casual dinner along with fresh fruit. And they nibble on them all day. Traditionally, biscotti are dunked into wine (usually a sweet wine, a Vin Santo), cappuccino, caffè latte or café au lait while you eat them. But some people (I'm one) like them best dry—the drier the better.

To make a terrific dessert, break up some biscotti in individual dessert bowls, top each bowl with a scoop of vanilla ice cream, and pour a few tablespoons of rum, brandy, or Grand Marnier over the ice cream. Place the bottle of rum, brandy, or Grand Marnier on the table for those who want more.

Occasionally, I hear someone say, "These biscotti are too hard." I like them this way. However, if you would like them less hard, although still dry and crisp, this is what you should do. Put them in a brown paper bag, twist the top closed, and let them stand at room temperature for 1 to 3 days (depending on the humidity).

Barbara's Milk Chocolate Biscotti

ABOUT 50 COOKIES

Gianni Versace, one of the world's leading fashion designers, has a magnificent ocean-front villa here in Miami Beach. A few weeks ago I met his handsome and talented young chef, Donato De Santis. Donato called me recently and happened to mention that they were having a dinner party that night. I asked what he was serving for dessert. He said, "Crème brûlée with fresh berries." I asked if he would like some of my biscotti to serve with it. (It seems that while I was writing this book I always had a kitchen full of biscotti.) He said that he would love it. I drove over and delivered a pretty-good-sized box of biscotti.

The villa is *magnifico*. *Splendido*. Gorgeous colorful Italian tiles and hand-carved dark wood wherever I looked. The kitchen is a dream. Very large with more colorful tiles and a Garland range. The kitchen cabinets have clear glass doors that display solid-white china. A beautiful fresh tomato sauce for pasta was on the stove, and a large tray of luscious diced and sliced fresh vegetables was ready nearby. (Donato served me cranberry juice.)

Just seeing it all was a treat, but it was more of a treat when Donato saw the biscotti and said, "They are beautiful. I can't make them as long as these are. I try to, but they fall apart."

Not these. These don't fall apart. I told Donato I would give him the recipe. (Actually, two recipes. The biscotti I brought were these chocolate ones and Lake Como Biscotti, page 34.)

This recipe came about when my friend Barbara Lazaroff said, "Please make a cookie with milk chocolate—I love milk chocolate." Because of the combination of milk chocolate and cocoa in this recipe, everybody loves them.

They are very dark chocolate with a light/airy/crisp/porous/crunchy texture that is divine. They are extra long and extra thin.

After you mix and shape the dough it will have to spend about 2 hours in the freezer before it is baked (it can stay longer). There are two bakings, which will total about 1 hour and 40 minutes.

These are this season's specialty chez moi.

7 ounces (1⅓ cups) whole blanched (skinned) almonds
7 ounces milk chocolate (I use Hershey's Symphony bar.)
1¾ cups sifted unbleached flour
1 teaspoon baking soda
⅛ teaspoon salt
⅓ cup unsweetened cocoa powder (I use a Dutch-process cocoa.)
1 cup granulated sugar
4 eggs graded "large"
1 teaspoon vanilla extract

Toast the almonds in a shallow pan in a preheated 350-degree oven for 12 to 15 minutes, until lightly colored, shaking the pan once or twice. You can tell when they are done by the strong smell of toasted almonds when you open the oven door. Set aside to cool.

Cut or break the chocolate into small pieces and place it in the bowl of a food processor fitted with the metal chopping blade. Let stand.

Sift together the flour, baking soda, salt, cocoa, and sugar. Add about a cup of these sifted ingredients to the chocolate. Process for about 30 seconds, or until the chocolate is fine and powdery.

In a large bowl mix together the processed ingredients with the remaining sifted dry ingredients. Stir in the almonds.

In a small bowl beat the eggs with the vanilla just to mix. With a large rubber or wooden spatula stir the egg mixture into the dry ingredients. You might think there is not enough liquid, but there is—just keep stirring.

Now place two 20-inch lengths of plastic wrap on the work surface.

In order to shape two loaves, spoon a strip of the dough down the middle of each piece of plastic wrap. Each strip should be 13 to 14 inches long. Flatten the tops with the bottom of a wet spoon. Lift the two long sides of the plastic wrap (hold them together as close as possible to the dough—touching the dough) and—with your hands—press on the plastic wrap to smooth the dough and shape it into an even strip 14 to 15 inches long, 2½ to 3 inches wide, and ¾ inch thick (no thicker), with squared ends. If the strips of dough are thicker than they should be, the baked strips will not slice neatly.

Transfer to a cookie sheet and place in the freezer for about 2 hours (or as much longer as you wish), until firm enough to be unwrapped.

To bake, adjust two racks to divide the oven into thirds. Preheat oven to 300 degrees. Line two large cookie sheets with baking parchment or aluminum foil, shiny side up.

To transfer the frozen dough to the sheets (the dough might still be a bit sticky; if so, it is OK), open the two long sides of plastic wrap on top of one strip of dough and turn the dough upside down on the lined sheet, placing it diagonally on the sheet. Slowly peel off the plastic wrap. Repeat with the second strip and the second sheet.

Bake for 1 hour, reversing the sheets top to bottom and front to back once during baking to insure even baking. During baking the strips will spread out (7 to 8 inches wide).

After 1 hour of baking reduce the oven temperature to 275 degrees and remove the sheets from the oven. Immediately, with a wide, metal spatula release a strip from the parchment or foil and place it on a board. Repeat with the second strip.

Use a pot holder or a folded towel to hold the hot strip in place, and use a serrated French bread knife to cut the strip crosswise into slices ½ to ¾ inch wide.

Repeat with the second strip. Place the slices, standing upright, on unlined cookie sheets with a little space between them.

Bake for 40 minutes, reversing the sheets top to bottom and front to back once during baking.

Let cool and store in an airtight container.

Gingerful Biscotti

This is the recipe that made me decide to write another book.

These are especially appropriate during the holiday season because of their spicy and festive flavor. (But holidays or not, these are sensational!) They make a fantastic gift (give the recipe too). They last very well and they mail very well. I layer them with plastic bubble wrap in a Rubbermaid freezer box, and then I put that in a larger cardboard box with crumpled newspaper to fill in the empty space between the boxes.

The pepper should preferably be freshly ground, and it must be fine. If you don't have a pepper mill that grinds very fine, grind it in a blender until it is powdery. If you must use pepper that you buy already ground, it is best to use only ¾ to 1 teaspoon since it packs down while standing.

4 ounces (1 loosely packed cup) crystallized ginger (see Note)
7 ounces (1¼ cups) blanched (skinned) or unblanched whole almonds
3 cups sifted unbleached flour
¾ teaspoon baking soda
¾ teaspoon baking powder
¼ teaspoon salt
1¼ teaspoons finely ground white pepper (preferably freshly ground)
1 teaspoon ground ginger
½ teaspoon ground cinnamon
½ teaspoon ground mustard powder
¼ teaspoon ground cloves
½ cup granulated sugar
3 eggs graded "large"
½ cup mild honey

I find it easiest to cut ginger with scissors. Cut it into thin slices and then crosswise to make pieces about the size of small green peas; set aside. (Yes, cutting ginger is boring.)

Toast the almonds in a shallow pan in a 350-degree oven for 12 to 15 minutes, until lightly colored, stirring once during toasting. Set aside to cool.

Into a large bowl strain or sift together—just to mix—the flour, baking soda, baking powder, salt, pepper, ground ginger, cinnamon, mustard, cloves, and sugar. Stir in the crystallized ginger, then the nuts. In a small bowl beat the eggs and honey to mix and add to the dry ingredients. Stir (preferably with a large rubber spatula) until the dry ingredients are completely moistened.

Place two 18- to 20-inch lengths of plastic wrap on a work surface. You will form two strips of the dough, one on each piece of plastic wrap. Spoon half of the dough by heaping tablespoonfuls in the mid-dle—down the length—of each piece of plastic wrap, to form strips about 13 inches long. Flatten the tops slightly by dipping a large spoon into water and pressing down on the dough with the wet spoon. Rewet the spoon often.

Lift the two long sides of one piece of plastic wrap, bring the sides together on top of the dough, and, with your hands, press on the plastic wrap to smooth the dough and shape it into an even strip about 13 to 14 inches long, 2½ to 3½ inches wide, and about ¾ inch thick (no thicker). Shape both strips and place them on a cookie sheet.

(If there is an air bubble on the side of the dough, pierce a small hole in the plastic wrap with the tip of a sharp knife to allow the air to escape. Then press on the plastic wrap to spread the dough into that space.)

Place the cookie sheet with the strips of dough in the freezer for at least an hour or until firm enough to unwrap (or as much longer as you wish).

To bake, adjust two racks to divide the oven into thirds and pre-heat oven to 300 degrees. Line two large cookie sheets with baking parchment or aluminum foil, shiny side up.

To transfer the strips of dough to the sheets, open the two long sides of plastic wrap on top of one strip of dough and turn the dough upside down onto the lined cookie sheet, placing it diagonally on the sheet. Slowly peel off the plastic wrap. Repeat with the second strip of dough and the second cookie sheet.

Bake for 50 minutes, reversing the sheets top to bottom and front to back once during baking to insure even baking. These will turn quite dark during baking.

Then reduce the temperature to 275 degrees and remove the sheets from the oven. Immediately—carefully and gently—peel the parchment or foil away from the backs of the strips and place them on a large cutting board. Slice the strips while they are still very hot. Use a pot holder or a folded towel to hold a strip in place. Use a serrated French bread knife. Slice on an angle; the sharper the angle, the longer the cookies, and the more difficult it will be to slice them very thin—but you can do it, and they will be gorgeous. Cut them about ¼ to ⅓ inch wide.

Place the slices on a cut side, touching each other, on the cookie sheets. Bake at 275 degrees for about 25 minutes.

(If you bake one sheet alone they will bake in a bit less time. This is true of all cookies, but seems especially noticeable with these.)

Because these are so thin it is not necessary to turn them upside down during this second baking; they bake evenly without it.

Reverse the sheets top to bottom and front to back once during baking. Bake just until dry. (You have to cool one to know if it is crisp.) Do not overbake.

When done, cool and then store in an airtight container.

To serve, these are especially attractive standing upright in a wide, clear glass.

Note: This is a lot of ginger. It's the way I like it—I love it. But use less if you prefer.

P.S. When I make these, the slices are 7 to 8 inches long—but I've had a lot of experience with them. I've made these many, many times. But even if the slices are short they taste just as wonderful.

Chocolate Chip and Almond Biscotti

ABOUT 40 BISCOTTI

Irresistible. Awesome. With a huge, tremendous amount of chocolate chips. Chocolate chips never had it so good.

6 ounces (1¼ cups) whole blanched
    (skinned) almonds
2 cups sifted unbleached flour
½ teaspoon baking soda
½ teaspoon baking powder
⅛ teaspoon salt
1 cup minus 2 tablespoons granulated
    sugar
12 ounces (2 cups) semisweet chocolate
    morsels
2 eggs graded "large"
1 teaspoon vanilla extract
2 tablespoons whiskey or brandy

First toast the almonds in a single layer in a shallow pan in a 350-degree oven for 12 to 15 minutes, shaking the pan a few times, until the almonds are lightly colored and have a delicious smell of toasted almonds when you open the oven door. Set aside to cool.

Adjust two racks to divide the oven into thirds and preheat oven to 375 degrees. If possible, use cookie sheets with two or three flat edges; otherwise use any sheets upside down. Line the sheets with baking parchment or aluminum foil, shiny side up, and set aside.

Sift together into a large bowl (preferably one with flared rather than straight sides) the flour, baking soda, baking powder, and salt. Add the sugar and stir to mix.

Place about ½ cup of these dry ingredients in the bowl of a food processor fitted with the metal chopping blade. Add about ½ cup of the toasted almonds and process for about 30 seconds, until the nuts are fine and powdery.

Add the processed mixture to the sifted ingredients in the large bowl. Add the remaining toasted almonds and the chocolate morsels; stir to mix.

In a small bowl beat the eggs with the vanilla and whiskey or brandy, just to mix.

Add the egg mixture to the dry ingredients and stir until the dry ingredients are moistened (I stir with a large rubber spatula). Be patient.

Place a length of baking parchment or wax paper on the counter next to the sink. Turn the dough out onto the parchment or wax paper. Wet your hands with cold water—do not dry them—and press the dough into a round mound.

With a long, heavy, sharp knife cut the dough into equal quarters.

Continue to wet your hands as you form each piece of dough into a strip about 9 inches long, 2 to 2½ inches wide, and about ½ inch high (you will press, not roll, the dough into shape). The ends of the strips should be rounded rather than squared.

Place two strips crosswise on each of the lined sheets.

Bake for 25 minutes, reversing the sheets top to bottom and front to back once during baking.

Remove the sheets from the oven and slide the parchment or foil off the sheets. With a wide metal spatula transfer the baked strips to a large cutting board and let them cool for 20 minutes.

Reduce the oven temperature to 275 degrees.

With a serrated French bread knife, carefully cut on a sharp angle into slices about ½ inch wide. This is tricky. Cut slowly with a sawing motion.

Place the slices, cut side down, on the two unlined sheets.

Bake the two sheets, turning the slices upside down (ouch—they're hot) and reversing the sheets top to bottom and front to back once during baking.

Bake for 25 to 30 minutes (depending on the thickness of the biscotti).

Turn the oven heat off, open the oven door, and let the biscotti cool in the oven.

When cool, store in an airtight container.

Bittersweet Chocolate Biscotti

Extra hard and crunchy—thicker than most—and especially dark and delicious, made with chocolate and cocoa.

After you mix and shape the dough it will have to spend 45 minutes in the freezer before it is baked. It will then be baked twice for a total of 1 hour and 45 minutes.

ABOUT 36 BISCOTTI

9 ounces (generous 2 cups) whole blanched (skinned) almonds
6 ounces semisweet chocolate
1¾ cups sifted unbleached flour
1 teaspoon baking soda
⅛ teaspoon salt
⅓ cup unsweetened cocoa powder
1 tablespoon instant espresso powder (I use Medaglia D'Oro.)
½ cup granulated sugar
3 eggs plus 1 egg white graded "large"
½ packed cup light brown sugar
1 teaspoon vanilla extract
Scant ½ teaspoon almond extract or ¼ teaspoon bitter almond extract

First toast the almonds: Preheat the oven to 375 degrees and bake the almonds in a wide, shallow pan in the center of the oven, stirring once or twice, for 12 or 13 minutes, until very lightly colored. Set aside to cool.

Chop or break the chocolate into small pieces and place in the bowl of a food processor fitted with the metal chopping blade. Let stand.

Sift together into a large bowl the flour, baking soda, salt, cocoa, espresso, and granulated sugar.

Add about ½ cup of the sifted dry ingredients and about ½ cup of the almonds to the chocolate. Process for about 30 seconds, until the chocolate and nuts are fine and powdery.

Add the processed ingredients to the remaining sifted dry ingredients and stir to mix. Stir in the remaining almonds; set aside.

Biscotti and Zwieback • 25

In a small bowl beat the eggs and egg white, brown sugar, vanilla, and almond extract until mixed.

Stir the egg mixture into the dry ingredients (you will think there's not enough liquid, but it will be OK). I use a large rubber spatula and push the ingredients together).

Now place two 15- to 20-inch lengths of plastic wrap on the work surface.

The dough will be thick and sticky. You will form a strip of it on each piece of the plastic wrap. Spoon half the dough in the middle—down the length—of one piece of plastic wrap to form a strip 12 inches long.

Lift the two long sides of the plastic wrap, bring them together on top of the dough, and, with your hands, press on the plastic wrap to smooth the dough and shape it into an even strip 12 inches long, 3 inches wide, and ¾ inch high, with squared ends.

Repeat to form the second strip.

Place the strips on a cookie sheet and put in the freezer for about 45 minutes or until firm.

To bake, adjust two racks to divide the oven into thirds and preheat oven to 300 degrees. Line two cookie sheets with baking parchment.

Open the two long sides of the plastic wrap on one strip of dough and turn the dough upside down on a lined sheet, placing it diagonally on the sheet; slowly peel off the plastic wrap. Repeat with the second strip and the second cookie sheet.

Bake for 1 hour, reversing the sheets top to bottom and front to back once during baking to insure even baking.

After one hour reduce the temperature to 275 degrees and remove the sheets from the oven. Immediately, while very hot, peel the parchment away from the back of a strip and place it right side up on a cutting board.

Use a pot holder or folded kitchen towel to hold the hot strip, and use a serrated French bread knife to cut it with. Cut across the strip, either straight across or on an angle (straight across is easier), cutting slices about ¾ inch wide.

Place the slices, standing upright, on a cookie sheet.

Repeat with the second strip.

Bake at 275 degrees for about 45 minutes, until completely dry. Reverse the sheets top to bottom and front to back once during baking.

Cool and store in an airtight container.

Multigrain and Seed Biscotti

ABOUT 65 THIN
COOKIES

Hard, crunchy, and loaded with a shopping cart full of things from a health food store. I made these up recently when I went to a spa (Canyon Ranch in Arizona) where the food was wonderful and I was inspired. I made them in the demonstration kitchen at the spa.

After you mix and shape the dough, it has to wait about 45 minutes in the freezer before you bake it. Then there are two bakings that total about 1 hour and 20 minutes.

Some of my friends who work out every day at a gym, and are deeply involved with lean bodies and strict diets, love these so much that they say they could eat them all day long, every day. But even people who are not thinking about health food are wild about them. Incidentally, they are great for breakfast with espresso or cappuccino.

1 cup sifted unbleached flour
1¼ cups sifted whole wheat flour (Any flour that is too coarse to go through the sifter should be stirred into the sifted part.)
1½ teaspoons baking powder
¼ teaspoon salt
1 teaspoon finely ground white or black pepper (preferably freshly ground)
1½ teaspoons ground ginger
⅓ cup unsifted rye flour
¼ cup oat bran
¼ cup cornmeal
⅓ cup untoasted, unsalted sunflower seeds
¼ cup sesame seeds
¼ cup flax seeds
⅓ cup untoasted, unsalted pumpkin seeds
9 ounces (2 cups) pignolias (pine nuts)

3 eggs graded "large"
½ cup mild honey
½ firmly packed cup light brown sugar

Sift together into a large bowl the unbleached flour, whole wheat flour, baking powder, salt, pepper, and ginger (any of the whole wheat flour that is too coarse to go through the sifter should be stirred back into the sifted ingredients).

Add the rye flour, oat bran, cornmeal, sunflower seeds, sesame seeds, flax seeds, pumpkin seeds, and pignolias; stir until thoroughly mixed.

In a small bowl beat the eggs, honey, and brown sugar until mixed. Add the egg mixture to the dry ingredients and stir until thoroughly mixed.

Now place two 20-inch lengths of plastic wrap on the work surface.

On each piece of plastic wrap spoon a strip of the dough (using half of the dough) down the middle. Each strip should be about 14 inches long. Lift the two long sides of the plastic wrap, bring them together on top of the dough (hold them together as close as possible to the dough, touching the dough), and, with your hands, press on the plastic wrap to smooth the dough and shape it into an even strip about 15 inches long, 2½ to 3 inches wide, and ¾ inch thick (no thicker!). Turn it all upside down and smooth the other side.

Place both strips on a cookie sheet in the freezer for about 45 minutes, until the dough is firm enough to be unwrapped.

To bake, adjust two racks to divide the oven into thirds and preheat oven to 300 degrees. Line two large cookie sheets with baking parchment.

To transfer the cold dough to the sheets, open the long sides of plastic wrap on top of one strip and turn the dough upside down onto a lined sheet, placing it diagonally on the sheet. Slowly peel off the plastic wrap. Repeat with the second strip and the second sheet.

Bake for 50 minutes, reversing the sheets top to bottom and front to back once during baking (these will hold their shape nicely during baking).

After 50 minutes of baking, reduce the temperature to 275 degrees and remove the sheets from the oven.

Immediately, peel the parchment away from the back of one strip and place the strip on a cutting board.

Use a pot holder or a folded towel to hold the hot strip in place, and use a serrated French bread knife or a long, thin, sharp knife (a ham slicer) to cut the strip on an angle into slices $\frac{1}{3}$ inch wide. With the right knife, these will slice beautifully.

Repeat with the second strip.

Place the slices, cut side down, on unlined cookie sheets.

Bake for 30 minutes at 275 degrees. Once, during baking, turn the slices upside down and reverse the sheets top to bottom and front to back.

These should not darken much during the second baking. Watch them carefully; do not overbake. To test for doneness, cool one quickly in the freezer; if it is completely dried and crisp, it is done.

Cool and then store in airtight containers.

Note: All of these seeds and grains should be stored in the freezer or refrigerator.

Palm Beach Biscotti

My friend Lisette Ackerberg sent me this wonderful recipe from Palm Beach. First, the easy dough is baked in two loaf pans, then the loaves are cooled and frozen (for as long as you wish), then sliced thin and baked again. Palm Beach hostesses compete to see who can serve the thinnest biscotti.

The slices are like sweet melba toast loaded with pecans (whole halves if possible). They are plain but are chic and classy—a pale golden color, gorgeous.

You will need two loaf pans. The ones I use have a 6-cup capacity and measure 8½ by 4½ by 2¾ inches. You could easily use pans that are a little larger, but preferably not much smaller.

1¾ cups sifted unbleached flour
Scant ½ teaspoon salt
½ teaspoon baking powder
4 ounces (1 stick) unsalted butter
1 teaspoon vanilla extract
1½ cups granulated sugar
4 eggs graded "large"
10 ounces (3 cups) pecan halves (or large pieces if necessary)

Adjust an oven rack one-third up from the bottom of the oven and preheat oven to 350 degrees. Butter two loaf pans with about a 6-cup capacity (see above). Dust the pans thoroughly with fine, dry bread crumbs and invert over paper to remove excess, but you should leave a rather generous coating. Set the pans aside.

Sift together the flour, salt, and baking powder; set aside.

In the large bowl of an electric mixer beat the butter until soft. Beat in the vanilla, then the sugar, then the eggs, one at a time. Add the sifted dry ingredients and beat on low speed, scraping the bowl as necessary with a rubber spatula and beating only until incorporated. Remove the bowl from the mixer and stir in the nuts.

You will have about 5 cups of batter. Place half (2½ cups) in each pan; the pans will be less than half full. Smooth the tops. Then, with the bottom of a large spoon, form a deep trench down the length of each pan—this will help to prevent a high mound in the middle of each loaf.

Bake both pans on the same rack for about 55 minutes, reversing the pans front to back after about 30 minutes to insure even baking, until a cake tester inserted in the middle comes out clean. The pans will only be about two-thirds full.

Remove the pans from the oven. The baked loaves have a crust on top, which would crumble when you slice them. To prevent that, wet and wring out a paper towel (it should remain wet but not dripping). Open the towel, fold it in half, and place it directly on top of (touching) one of the loaves. Then cover the top of the pan with aluminum foil and fold the foil down over the sides of the pan to keep the steam in. Repeat with the second loaf.

Let the cakes cool in the pans.

Cover a pan with a small cake rack and invert the pan and rack. Remove the pan. With your hands, carefully turn the loaf right side up without the foil and damp paper towel. It will be a shallow loaf.

Repeat with the second loaf. Wrap the loaves in plastic wrap.

Freeze for several hours or as much longer as you wish.

For the second baking adjust two racks to divide the oven into thirds and preheat oven to 325 degrees.

Place a frozen loaf right side up on a cutting board. Use a long, thin knife with a sharp, straight blade. (The knife I use is called a ham slicer—or use a serrated knife.) Cut slowly and carefully. If the loaf is too hard to slice neatly (depending on the temperature in your freezer), just wait a few minutes and try again. The slices should be ¼ inch thick (thin).

Place the slices, cut side down, right next to each other on an unlined cookie sheet. Repeat with the second loaf, or save that for some other time if you wish.

Bake two sheets at a time. Reverse the sheets top to bottom and front to back frequently during baking to insure even browning. Bake until dry and a pale golden color. It will take 15 to 25 minutes, depending on the thickness. Do not overbake. Watch them carefully; as soon as they start to color they can very suddenly become too dark. Remove the slices one at a time when they are ready. Transfer them to a rack or place them on paper towels or a large brown paper bag.

Let cool and store in an airtight container.

Variations

Pecan and Ginger Slices: With scissors, cut crystallized ginger into thin strips and then cut crosswise to make pieces the size of very small peas. Use about 2½ ounces (½ cup) of the ginger, mixed into half the dough, to make one loaf. These are divine.

Pecan, Pistachio, and Lemon Slices: Finely grate the rind of 3 large, cold, firm lemons. Stir it into half the prepared dough, and then stir in about ⅓ cup unsalted green pistachio nuts to make one loaf.

Lake Como Biscotti

ABOUT 50 BISCOTTI

These are like the biscotti we had at the luxurious and regal Villa D'Este hotel on the shore of Lake Como in Italy. We planned to spend one day on a boat, and the hotel packed a picnic lunch for us. We had prosciutto, fruit, wonderful bread (it was a *ciabatta,* with a divine dense and chewy consistency), vegetable salads, red wine—and these biscotti. Although I would love to be at the Villa D'Este right now, there is a special thrill—one the hotel can't match—in making these myself in my own kitchen.

Question: "Why are these better than the ones we had in Italy?"

Answer: "Because these are now."

9 ounces (2 cups) whole blanched (skinned) almonds
2 cups sifted unbleached flour
½ teaspoon baking soda
½ teaspoon baking powder
⅛ teaspoon salt
1 cup minus 2 tablespoons granulated sugar
2 eggs graded "large"
Finely grated rind of 1 large and firm lemon
1 tablespoon plus 1½ teaspoons lemon juice
Scant ½ teaspoon almond extract or ¼ teaspoon bitter almond
   extract

First toast the almonds in a shallow pan in a 350-degree oven for 12 to 15 minutes, shaking the pan a few times, until the almonds are lightly colored and have a strong smell of toasted almonds. Set aside to cool.

Adjust two racks to divide the oven into thirds and preheat oven to 375 degrees. If possible, use a cookie sheet that has two or three flat sides; otherwise, use any sheet upside down. Line the sheet with baking parchment or aluminum foil, shiny side up, and set aside.

Sift together into a large bowl (see Note) the flour, baking soda, baking powder, and salt. Add the sugar and stir to mix. Place about ½ cup of these ingredients in the bowl of a food processor fitted with the metal chopping blade. Add about ½ cup of the toasted almonds and process for about 30 seconds, until the nuts are fine and powdery.

Add the processed mixture and the remaining nuts to the sifted ingredients in the large bowl; stir to mix.

In a small bowl, with a beater or a whisk, beat the eggs with the rind, juice, and almond extract just to mix.

Add the egg mixture to the dry ingredients and stir to mix. Stir and stir and stir (I stir with a large rubber spatula) until the dry ingredients are finally moistened. Be patient.

Lightly flour a large board or a countertop and turn the dough out onto the floured area. Sprinkle a bit of flour over the top. Shape the dough into a mound. With a long, sharp knife cut it into equal quarters.

Flour the surface as necessary, and flour your hands lightly. One at a time, roll the pieces of dough under your hands to form long and narrow sausage shapes (about 10 inches long and 1 inch wide). The rolls of dough should be firm and compact or it will be difficult to slice them after they are baked. With a pastry brush, brush off any loose flour. Do not flatten the tops.

Place all four rolled loaves crosswise on the lined sheet. They should be about 2 inches apart.

Bake the loaves on the upper rack for about 20 minutes, reversing the sheet front to back once during baking. After 20 minutes they should be lightly colored and should feel almost firm. Remove from the oven.

Reduce the oven temperature to 275 degrees.

Slide the parchment or foil off the sheet. With a spatula transfer the loaves to a cutting board.

Hold a hot loaf with a pot holder or a folded towel and, with a serrated French bread knife, carefully cut the loaf on a sharp angle into slices ½ to ¾ inch wide. Cut with a sawing motion. Continue to cut all four loaves into slices.

Place the slices, cut side down, on two unlined cookie sheets.

Bake the two sheets for 35 to 40 minutes, turning the slices upside down and reversing the sheets top to bottom and front to back once during baking.

After 35 to 40 minutes the slices should be a pale honey color on both sides. Do not underbake. Remove from the oven. Let stand until cool.

Store in an airtight container.

Note: The ingredients will go together a bit more easily in a bowl with flared sides rather than in a bowl with straight sides.

SoBe* Biscotti

35 TO 45 SLICES

The slices are wonderfully hard and dry, and the fruit is deliciously chewy. Great! Made with almonds, raisins, sour cherries, and lemon rind. The dough is baked in a loaf pan, then cooled and refrigerated for several hours or overnight, then sliced and baked again for about half an hour.

Mixing the ingredients for this recipe involves an unusual procedure.

The slices are a very nice shape if you use a loaf pan that measures 10½ by 3¾ by 3¼ inches and has an 8-cup capacity. You can also use a pan 8½ by 4½ by 2¾ with a 6-cup capacity, or any pan that is close to either size.

4 ounces (1½ cups) thin-sliced almonds
4 eggs graded "large," separated
1 teaspoon fresh lemon juice (Grate the rind of the lemon before
   you squeeze the juice, to use below.)
¾ cup granulated sugar
1 teaspoon vanilla extract
¼ teaspoon salt
Finely grated rind of 1 cold and firm lemon
2 cups sifted unbleached flour
½ cup raisins
½ cup dried pitted sour cherries

Adjust a rack to the center of the oven and preheat oven to 350 degrees. Butter a loaf pan with a 6- or 8-cup capacity (see above). Then line the pan with aluminum foil as follows: Measure the bottom of the pan and fold or cut two pieces of foil, one for the length and both sides and another for the width and both sides. Place the pan upside down and place the foil over the pan, shaping each piece to fit.

* South Beach

Remove the foil. Turn the pan right side up. Place one piece of foil in the pan, pressing it into place. Butter the bottom of the foil. Place the other piece of foil in the pan, pressing it into place (there will be a double thickness on the bottom of the pan). Butter the foil all over, then dust all over with fine dry bread crumbs, inverting over paper to shake out excess. Set the pan aside.

Toast the almonds by placing them in a wide, shallow pan in a 350-degree oven. Bake for about 13 minutes, stirring occasionally, until golden in color. Set aside.

In the small bowl of an electric mixer beat the egg whites (reserve the yolks) with the lemon juice until they just barely hold a straight point when the beaters are raised. Gradually beat in ¼ cup of the sugar (reserve remaining ½ cup sugar) and then beat at high speed until the whites hold a firm peak when the beaters are raised. Transfer to a larger bowl and set aside.

In a small bowl beat the yolks with the vanilla and salt until slightly lighter in color. Stir in the lemon rind.

Fold the yolks into the whites. Fold in the reserved ½ cup sugar. Fold in the flour and then fold in the almonds, raisins, and cherries. (It will be a thick and stiff mixture and you will think there are too many dry ingredients, and/or not enough eggs—folding will deflate the beaten whites—but it will be OK.)

Turn the mixture into the prepared pan. Smooth the top. Then, with the bottom of a spoon, make a slight trench down the length of a loaf (it will help to prevent a too-high mound in the middle, although there will be a small mound anyway).

Bake for 30 minutes, then cover the top of the pan with a piece of foil large enough to fold down securely over the sides of the pan. (This will keep the steam in the pan so that a hard crust doesn't form on top of the loaf. A crust would make it difficult to slice.) Continue to bake for 30 to 40 minutes more, until a cake tester gently inserted in the middle comes out dry. (Remove the foil briefly to test and then replace it. The top will be very pale.) Total baking time is one hour in the narrower pan and 1 hour and 10 minutes in the wider pan.

Remove the cake from the oven but do not remove the foil from the top of the pan. Let the cake cool for 30 minutes. Then cover with a small rack or a small board and invert the pan and rack or board. Remove the pan, and with your hands, carefully turn the cake right side up (it will still be hot). Immediately wrap the hot cake in aluminum foil. Let cool, and then refrigerate for several hours or longer.

When you are ready to slice the loaf and bake the slices, adjust two racks to divide the oven into thirds and preheat oven to 300 degrees.

Use either a serrated French bread knife or a knife with a long, straight, thin, sharp blade. Cut the loaf into ¼-inch slices. If the loaf is too firm let it stand at room temperature for 5 to 10 minutes. Place the slices, cut side down, on unbuttered, unlined cookie sheets and bake two sheets at a time for about 30 minutes, depending on the thickness of the slices. Once during baking, reverse the sheets top to bottom and front to back. Bake only until the slices are lightly colored (don't let them really brown—they won't taste as good). If the slices are not quite thin enough—if they are not browning on both sides equally—turn the slices upside down once during baking. Remove the slices one at a time as they are done (I just place them on a large brown paper bag or on paper towels).

Cool and then store in an airtight container.

Note: If you wish, this can be made with 1 cup raisins or 1 cup cherries instead of ½ cup of each.

Macadamia Shortbread Biscotti

Irresistible, simple, elegant, extravagant—and sexy. They look like the usual biscotti, but they are something else. They are shortbread loaded with the most luxurious nuts of all.

These must be handled very carefully—they are fragile. Too fragile to mail (I found out the hard way).

20 TO 24 COOKIES

4 ounces (1 stick) unsalted butter
1 teaspoon vanilla extract
$^{1}/_{2}$ teaspoon almond extract or $^{1}/_{4}$ teaspoon bitter almond extract
$^{1}/_{4}$ teaspoon salt
$^{1}/_{2}$ cup granulated sugar
1 egg graded "large"
1$^{1}/_{4}$ cups sifted unbleached flour
7$^{1}/_{2}$ ounces (about 1$^{1}/_{2}$ cups) roasted and lightly salted whole
    macadamia nuts (I use the Mauna Loa nuts in a jar—they are
    roasted and salted.)

Adjust a rack high in the oven (these have a tendency to become too dark on the bottom if they are baked lower). The rack can be one-fourth to one-third down from the top. Preheat oven to 350 degrees. Use a flat-sided cookie sheet, or use any other sheet upside down. Line the sheet with baking parchment or aluminum foil, shiny side up.

In the small bowl of an electric mixer beat the butter until soft. Beat in the vanilla and almond extracts, salt, and sugar. Then beat in the egg and, on low speed, gradually add the flour and beat only until incorporated. Remove the bowl from the mixer and, with a wooden spatula, stir in the nuts.

Work with half the dough at a time. Place it by heaping tablespoonfuls in a strip about 9 inches long down the middle of a piece of plastic wrap about 15 inches long. Lift the two long sides of the plastic wrap and bring them together on top of the strip. Then, pressing gently on the plastic wrap with your hands, shape the strip into a smooth loaf about 9 inches long, 2 inches wide, and 1 inch thick. Turn upside down and smooth the other side.

Repeat with the second half of the dough and a second length of plastic wrap.

Place them in the freezer for only 10 to 12 minutes (no longer), just so they will become nonsticky enough to be unwrapped.

Unwrap the packages of dough and place them across the sheet (not lengthwise) with plenty of space in the middle and on the ends. These will each spread out to 4 inches or more in width.

Bake for 25 minutes, reversing the sheet front to back once during baking. When done, the tops will be pale with golden spots and the edges will be slightly darker.

Remove from the oven and reduce temperature to 300 degrees.

The baked loaves will be fragile. Carefully slide the parchment or foil off the sheet onto a cutting board. The edges might be a bit too dark or too uneven; if so, without waiting, trim them slightly using a long and sharp knife.

Let the loaves wait 5 minutes before you slice them.

With a long, thin, sharp knife cut the loaves crosswise or on a slight angle into slices ¾ to 1 inch wide.

Carefully place the slices, standing upright, on the cookie sheet.

Be sure the oven temperature has reduced to 300 degrees. Bake for 25 minutes, reversing the sheet front to back once during baking. When done, the slices should be golden on the tops but only lightly colored on the cut sides. The end slices—and any thinner slices—will take less time. They should be removed one by one as they are ready.

Place the baked slices on a brown paper bag or on a double thickness of paper towels to cool.

Handle very carefully, and store in an airtight container.

Vanilla Bean and Lemon Zwieback

This is light, airy, and delicate. Actually, it's a sponge cake that's baked, sliced, and baked again.

You will need a fresh vanilla bean. If you have a choice, choose Tahitian.

To fold the beaten egg whites and the other ingredients together you will need a large rubber spatula and a large, wide bowl. And for the first baking you will need two loaf pans that measure about 9 by 5 by 3 inches.

To make this right, it's best if you know how to fold ingredients together without losing the air that was beaten in. Then it's a cinch.

1 fresh vanilla bean
1 cup granulated sugar
1 large cold and firm lemon (or two medium)
6 eggs graded "large"
1/4 teaspoon salt
2 cups sifted unbleached flour

Adjust a rack to the center of the oven and preheat oven to 325 degrees. Butter 2 loaf pans that measure about 9 by 5 by 3 inches. Dust them all over with fine dry bread crumbs. Turn upside down over paper to remove excess crumbs, then set the pans aside.

With scissors, trim the tough ends from the vanilla bean. Cut it crosswise into slices as narrow as possible. Put the slices and 1/4 cup of the sugar (reserve remaining 3/4 cup of sugar) in the bowl of a food processor fitted with the metal chopping blade and process for almost a minute until the vanilla is in tiny pieces. You will still see a few larger pieces, but that's OK. Set aside.

Grate the lemon rind and then squeeze the juice (you should have about 2 1/2 tablespoons of juice); set the rind and juice aside separately.

Separate the eggs, placing the yolks in the small bowl of an electric mixer and the whites in the large bowl of the mixer. Add the lemon juice to the yolks, then the vanilla sugar and ½ cup of the reserved sugar (reserve remaining ¼ cup sugar). Beat at high speed for about 10 minutes, until very pale and very thick (when you raise the beaters the mixture should fall slowly in a wide ribbon).

Remove the bowl from the mixer, and stir in the grated lemon rind. Set aside.

Add the salt to the egg whites and, with clean beaters, beat the whites briefly at medium speed and then at high speed until they hold a soft shape. On medium speed again, gradually add the remaining ¼ cup sugar. Beat at high speed again until the whites hold a straight peak when the beaters are raised—but not until stiff. Remove from the mixer.

Transfer the egg yolk mixture to a large, wide bowl. (It is easier to fold ingredients together properly in a wide bowl.) Sift the flour over the yolks. Then place the beaten whites on top of the flour.

With a large rubber spatula, fold the ingredients together only until all the flour is incorporated. Do not fold any more than necessary.

Turn equal amounts into the loaf pans. Smooth the tops. The pans will be only about half full.

Bake both pans on the same rack for 35 to 40 minutes, until the tops spring back when gently pressed with a fingertip and the cakes come away from the sides of the pans. (The cakes will not reach the tops of the pans.)

Remove the pans from the oven. Let stand for just a few minutes. Then cover a pan with a small rack, turn upside down, remove the pan, and, with your hands, turn the loaf right side up. Repeat with the second loaf. Let cool for a few hours.

For the second baking, adjust two racks to divide the oven into thirds and preheat oven to 275 degrees.

With a very thin and very sharp knife, first trim a very narrow slice off both short ends of a loaf. Then cut the loaf into slices about ½ inch wide. Repeat with the second loaf.

Place the slices, cut side down, on cookie sheets.

Bake for 40 to 50 minutes, reversing the sheets top to bottom and front to back once during baking and turning the slices upside down once during baking. They should bake until completely dry, but they should remain pale or only slightly colored.

Turn the oven heat off, open the oven door partway, and let the slices cool in the oven.

When cool, store in an airtight container.

CHOCOLATE CHIP
PEANUT BUTTER BARS

MIAMI BEACH PEANUT BARS

HEATH BAR
BROWNIES

Bar Cookies

SKINNY
PEANUT
BARS

PALM BEACH BROWNIES
WITH CHOCOLATE-COVERED
MINTS

PECAN PASSION

PECAN PASSION
BRANDIED FRUIT BARS
MACADAMIA AND COCONUT BARS
CREOLE PECAN PRALINE BARS
MIAMI BEACH PEANUT FLATS
PALM SPRINGS LEMON SQUARES WITH DATES
PENUCHE PECAN BARS
NAPA VALLEY ALMOND BARS
COCONUT AND WALNUT OATMEAL BARS
CHOCOLATE ON OATMEAL BARS
BITTERSWEET CHOCOLATE BROWNIES
JANE FREIMAN'S BROWNIES
HEATH BAR BROWNIES
PALM BEACH BROWNIES WITH
CHOCOLATE-COVERED MINTS
BALI HAI BROWNIES
SKINNY PEANUT BARS
MILK CHOCOLATE CHIP SKINNY PEANUT BARS
CHOCOLATE CHIP PEANUT BUTTER BARS

BAR COOKIES

I'm a Virgo. That might have something to do with the fact that when I make cookies I want them all to be exactly alike. If I'm making bar cookies in a pan—like brownies—I want them all to be absolutely the same size. That's a tough thing to do if you cut the bars in the pan with the tip of a small paring knife.

It's easy to do if you remove the baked cake from the pan in one piece (which is no problem if you do it my way) and then cut the bars with a long-bladed knife. It's easy and fun, and even if you're not a Virgo, you will like it. If you are a Virgo, you will love it.

If you don't care how they look, that's your business, in which case you can just butter the pan, then remove the cookies however you want.

But if you do care, when you are ready to cut the bars (after the cake has been cooled, and in some recipes, chilled) use a ruler and toothpicks to mark the cake. Then, use the right knife. That means one with a long, sharp blade. For some recipes it should be a serrated blade, and for others a thin, straight blade or a heavy straight blade. If one knife isn't working right, try another. Cut slowly and carefully.

When you see the cookies all lined up on a serving tray—all beautiful and delicious looking, all exactly the same—you'll see what I mean.

Pecan Passion

24 BARS

These are divine! Especially chewy and gooey and crisp-crunchy like the best butter-pecan-caramel candy. There is a shallow, dense chocolate layer on the bottom and a top layer of caramel loaded with toasted pecans.

This is from my friend Carole Kotkin. The recipe, called Turtle Bars, was in her food column in *The Miami Herald*. If I were going into the cookie business now this is one of the first recipes I would use.

First, toast the pecans for the top layer. Place them in a shallow pan in a 350-degree oven for about 10 minutes, stirring once or twice, until they have a strong smell of toasted pecans when you open the oven door. Set them aside.

You will need a sugar thermometer for testing the top layer.

BOTTOM LAYER

3 ounces (¾ stick) unsalted butter
½ firmly packed cup light brown sugar
⅛ teaspoon salt
½ teaspoon vanilla extract
1 egg graded "large"
¼ cup unsweetened cocoa powder (I use Dutch process.)
¼ cup sifted unbleached flour

Adjust a rack one-third up from the bottom of the oven and preheat oven to 375 degrees. You will need a 9-inch-square pan. Turn the pan upside down. Center a 12-inch square of aluminum foil, shiny side down, over the pan. Press down on the sides and corners with your hands to shape the foil to the pan. Remove the foil. Turn the pan right side up. Place the shaped foil in the pan. Press it into place all over. Press on the foil in the corners to make it as smooth as possible. (If the foil tears, start over again with a fresh piece.) Place a piece of butter (additional to that called for in the ingredients) in the pan, put it in the oven to melt, and then, with a piece of crumpled plastic wrap, spread the butter all over the bottom and sides; set the pan aside.

In a small pan on moderate heat melt the butter. Place it in the small bowl of an electric mixer. Add the sugar, salt, vanilla, and egg, and beat to mix. Beat in the cocoa and flour.

Place this thick chocolate mixture in a ribbon or in several mounds all over the bottom of the lined pan. With the bottom of a metal spoon, spread the mixture in an even layer. It will be a thin layer. It will level itself while baking.

Bake for about 15 minutes, until the shallow cake springs back when gently pressed with a fingertip.

Remove the pan from the oven and let stand. Now prepare the topping.

PECAN TOPPING
1 tablespoon dark rum or cognac
$^1\!/_3$ cup heavy (whipping) cream
3 ounces ($^3\!/_4$ stick) unsalted butter
$1^1\!/_2$ firmly packed cups light brown sugar
Scant $^1\!/_4$ teaspoon salt
$^1\!/_4$ cup dark corn syrup
7 ounces (2 cups) toasted pecan halves (See the introduction to this recipe.)

Add the rum or cognac to the cream; set aside.

In a heavy, 3-quart saucepan over moderate heat melt the butter. With a wooden spoon or spatula stir in the sugar, salt, and corn syrup. Stir over moderate heat until the mixture begins to boil all over the surface. Place a sugar thermometer in the pan and cook, stirring a few times, until the temperature reaches 250 degrees (this takes about 2 minutes of boiling). Watch it carefully—do not let it cook even a bit too long.

Remove from the heat and quickly stir in the cream mixture (the mixture will bubble up) and then the pecans.

Immediately pour the hot mixture over the bottom layer. Use a metal spoon or a fork to make the layer rather even and to adjust any nuts that are piled too high. Be sure that there are as many nuts in the corners as in the center.

Bake at 375 degrees for 25 minutes. Time this very carefully. If you bake it the least bit too long, it will become too hard.

Remove from the oven and let stand for at least a few hours, until completely cool. Then cover the pan with a flat board or a cookie sheet. Turn the pan and the board or sheet upside down. Remove the pan. Peel off the foil. (If you have trouble removing the foil, it simply means you did not let the pan cool long enough.) Cover with a piece of baking pan liner paper or wax paper and another board or cookie sheet and turn upside down again, leaving the cake right side up.

With a long, sharp, heavy knife cut the cake into quarters. Cut each quarter in half. Now you have 8 strips; cut each strip into 3 bars.

Store in an airtight box with wax paper between the layers. If you store these in the freezer or refrigerator, they must come to room temperature before serving.

Note: I have made these with walnuts in place of pecans and they were delicious.

Brandied Fruit Bars

32 BARS

These are almost solid brandied fruits with just barely enough batter to hold them together. They are luxurious, but not too rich or too sweet. This recipe came about quite by accident when I was doing too many things at once—I lost track—and unintentionally left the butter out of a recipe I was following (it happens).

The fruits should be cut up and marinated for at least three hours, or as much longer as you wish. (The brandied fruit is dynamite. In my kitchen it doesn't all make it to the fruit bars.)

1½ pounds (3 firmly packed cups) dried fruits (see below)
½ cup brandy, cognac, or dark rum
7 ounces (2 cups) pecan halves
1 cup sifted unbleached flour
½ teaspoon baking powder
¼ teaspoon salt
3 eggs graded "large"
1 cup granulated sugar

You can use any combination and any variety of dried fruits. I have been using dates, prunes, apricots, figs, raisins, and sour cherries. I use 4 ounces (½ packed cup) of each. You could also use dried peaches, pears, apples, and/or cranberries. It is important to use fruit that is soft and moist. If it is stale and hard, the soaking and the baking will not soften it. With scissors, cut all the fruits except the raisins, cherries, and cranberries into slices ¼ to ⅓ inch wide. Place all the fruits in a leak-proof jar (I use a glass jar with a hinged lid and a rubber ring around the lid). Add the brandy, cognac, or rum. Place the jar in a shallow bowl (to catch any leakage) and turn the jar occasionally, from top to bottom and from side to side, to keep all the fruits wet. Let stand for at least 3 hours, or as much longer as you wish.

Before baking, adjust a rack to the center of the oven and preheat oven to 350 degrees. Prepare a 9 by 13 by 2-inch pan as follows: Invert the pan and cover evenly with a 17-inch length of aluminum foil, shiny side down. With your hands, press down on the sides and corners of the foil to shape it to the pan. Remove the foil. Turn the pan right side up. Pour some water into the pan to wet it all over, and pour out all but about a tablespoon of the water (the wet pan helps to hold the foil in place). Place the shaped foil in the pan and carefully press it firmly into place all over. To butter the foil, place a piece of butter in the pan and put it in the oven. When the butter has melted, use a pastry brush or a piece of crumpled plastic wrap to spread the butter all over the foil. Let stand until cool and set, then dust the pan all over with fine dry bread crumbs. Turn the pan upside down over paper to shake out excess; set the pan aside.

Toast the pecans in a shallow pan in the oven, shaking the pan a few times, for about 10 minutes, or just until they are very hot and smell toasted. Set aside to cool.

Sift together the flour, baking powder, and salt; set aside.

In the large bowl of an electric mixer beat the eggs just to mix. Add the sugar and beat to mix, then add the sifted dry ingredients and beat only until mixed.

Remove the bowl from the mixer and, with a large rubber or wooden spatula, stir in the prepared fruits (and any of the brandy, cognac, or rum that wasn't absorbed) and the nuts.

Turn into the prepared pan, smooth the top, and bake for 45 minutes, reversing the pan front to back once during baking, until the top is richly browned and springs back when gently pressed with a fingertip.

Remove from the oven and let stand until cool. Then cover with a cookie sheet and turn the pan and the sheet upside down. Remove the pan and peel off the foil. Cover with another cookie sheet or anything flat and large enough and turn upside down again, leaving the cake right side up.

Before you cut the cake into bars it should be well chilled—even frozen—and if you cut it with a serrated French bread knife it will cut beautifully.

Cut the cake into quarters. Then cut each piece in half by cutting through the two long sides. Finally, cut each piece into 4 bars (each about 3¼ by 1 inch).

If you wish, wrap these individually in clear cellophane, wax paper, or aluminum foil, or package them in an airtight container with wax paper between the layers. You can also place them on a serving tray and cover with plastic wrap.

Notes

1. Since the brandied fruit lasts so long, it's great to have a jar of it on hand so that you can make the fruit bars whenever you want them without waiting for the fruit. (But hide the jar.)

2. I buy dried sour cherries from American Spoon Foods in Petoskey, Michigan (800-222-5886).

Macadamia and Coconut Bars

A buttery, brown sugar bottom layer is covered with a moist and chewy, almost caramel-like topping that is loaded with an extravagant amount of gorgeous, whole macadamia nuts and shredded coconut. Divine! And the most tempting kitchen smell ever.

32 BARS

BOTTOM LAYER

4 ounces (1 stick) unsalted butter
½ packed cup light brown sugar
1 egg graded "large"
¼ teaspoon salt
1¼ cups sifted unbleached flour

Adjust a rack to the center of the oven and preheat oven to 350 degrees. Prepare a 9 by 13 by 2-inch pan as follows: Turn the pan upside down. Center a 17-inch length of aluminum foil, shiny side down, over the pan. Press down on the sides and corners to shape the foil to fit the pan. Remove the foil. Run some tap water into the pan to wet it all over. Pour out all but about a tablespoonful of the water (the wet pan helps to hold the foil in place). Then place the foil in the pan and press it gently against the bottom and sides to fit the pan. To butter the foil, place a piece of butter (additional to that called for in the ingredients) in the pan and put the pan in the oven until the butter melts. Then, with a piece of crumpled plastic wrap, spread the butter all over the bottom and sides. Place the pan in the freezer or refrigerator (a cold pan will make it easier to form this bottom layer of dough).

In the small bowl of an electric mixer beat the butter until soft. Add the sugar and beat until mixed. Beat in the egg and salt, and then, on low speed, add the flour and beat only until incorporated.

To form the bottom layer, place the mixture by very small spoonfuls all over the bottom of the cold pan. Then, with floured fingertips, carefully, patiently, and slowly spread the dough all over the bottom of the pan. (It will be necessary to reflour your fingertips very often.) Form an even layer.

Bake for about 15 minutes, until set.

Remove the pan from the oven and let stand. Do not turn off the oven.

TOP LAYER

7 ounces (about 1½ cups) salted macadamia nuts
2 tablespoons sifted unbleached flour
Pinch of salt
½ teaspoon baking powder
2 eggs graded "large"
1 teaspoon vanilla extract
1 packed cup light brown sugar
6 ounces (about 2 packed cups) shredded coconut

Shake the nuts gently in a wide strainer to remove loose excess salt; set aside.

Sift together the flour, salt, and baking powder; set aside.

In the small bowl of an electric mixer beat the eggs, vanilla, and sugar until thoroughly mixed. Beat in the sifted ingredients. Remove the bowl from the mixer and stir in 1½ cups of the coconut (reserve remaining coconut) and the nuts.

The pan may still be warm or it may have cooled—either is OK.

Use a tablespoon to place the mixture evenly on top of the bottom layer. Then, with the bottom of the spoon, spread into a smooth layer (it will be a very thin layer), then sprinkle with the remaining 1 cup coconut.

Bake for 25 minutes, reversing the pan front to back once during baking, until the top is richly browned and a toothpick inserted in the middle comes out clean.

Remove from the oven. Let stand until cool. Then cover with a cookie sheet and turn upside down. Remove the pan and carefully peel off the foil. Cover with wax paper or baking pan liner paper and another cookie sheet or a cutting board and turn upside down again, leaving the cake right side up.

Refrigerate for a few hours or more, or place in the freezer for about an hour. Use a ruler and toothpicks to mark the cake into quarters. Use a long and heavy knife with a straight or serrated blade. Cut into quarters, then cut each quarter into 8 bars.

Either wrap individually in clear cellophane or wax paper, or place the bars in an airtight container with wax paper between the layers.

Creole Pecan Praline Bars

This is a very old recipe from New Orleans. It is so wonderful, I think you will make it again and again—I know I will. These are thin bars with a crisp, brown sugar shortbread base, completely covered with pecan halves and a praline-like topping.

32 OR MORE BARS

4 ounces (1 stick) unsalted butter
1/4 teaspoon salt
1 packed cup light brown sugar
2 cups sifted unbleached flour
9 ounces (2 1/2 cups) large pecan halves

Adjust a rack to the center of the oven and preheat oven to 350 degrees. Prepare a 9 by 13 by 2-inch pan as follows: Cut a piece of aluminum foil large enough to cover the bottom and sides of the pan. Turn the pan upside down. Center the foil over the pan with the shiny side down, and, with your hands, press down on the sides and corners to shape the foil to fit the pan. Remove the foil. Run some tap water into the pan to wet it all over. Pour out all but about a tablespoon of the water (the wet pan helps to hold the foil in place). Then place the foil in the pan and press it against the bottom and sides. Do not butter the foil.

In the large bowl of an electric mixer beat the butter until soft. Add the salt and sugar and beat to mix. Add the flour and beat for a minute or two, until the ingredients form tiny crumbs that will hold together when you press the mixture between your fingers.

Turn the mixture into the prepared pan. With your fingertips spread the mixture to form a level layer. Then, with your fingertips and with the palm of your hand, press down firmly on the mixture to form a compact layer.

Place the pecan halves touching each other—flat sides down—all in the same direction, to cover the bottom layer. Let stand.

TOPPING
6 ounces (1 1/2 sticks) unsalted butter

⅓ packed cup light brown sugar

In a saucepan with about a 4-cup capacity place the butter and sugar. Stir over high heat with a wooden spatula until the mixture comes to a hard boil all over the surface. Continue to stir over the heat for 30 seconds longer.

Then remove the pan from the heat and pour the hot mixture all over the pecans, trying to coat the entire surface.

Bake for 22 minutes.

Remove from the oven and let stand until cool.

Refrigerate for an hour or more. Then cover the pan with a cookie sheet. Turn the pan and cookie sheet upside down. Remove the pan and peel off the foil.

Then turn the cold and firm cake right side up on a cutting board.

First mark the cake into quarters using a ruler and toothpicks. Then, with a long, heavy, sharp knife cut the cake into quarters. Then cut each piece in half, cutting through the long sides. Finally, cut each piece into 4 strips (or, if you wish, cut into many more miniatures—they're delicious tiny).

Wrap the bars individually in clear cellophane, wax paper, or aluminum foil, or place them in an airtight container with wax paper between the layers. You can also place them on a serving tray and cover with plastic wrap.

These must come to room temperature before serving.

Miami Beach Peanut Flats

Thin and tender cookies, loaded with and covered with chopped salted peanuts. The combination of salted peanuts in a sweet brown sugar cookie is wonderful.

16 OR 32 BARS

6 ounces (1½ cups) salted peanuts
1 cup sifted unbleached flour
Pinch of salt
¼ teaspoon baking soda
½ teaspoon ground cinnamon
4 ounces (1 stick) unsalted butter
1 teaspoon vanilla extract
½ firmly packed cup light brown sugar
1 egg, graded "large"

Adjust a rack to the center of the oven and preheat oven to 325 degrees. Prepare a 15½ by 10½ by 1-inch jelly roll pan as follows: Turn the pan upside down. Center a 17½-inch length of aluminum foil, shiny side down, over the pan. Press down on the sides and corners of the foil to shape it to the pan. Remove the foil. Run some tap water into the pan to wet it all over. Pour out all but about a tablespoon of the water (the wet pan helps to hold the foil in place). Place the shaped foil in the pan and press gently all over to fit it to the pan. To butter the pan, place a piece of butter (additional to that called for in the ingredients) in the pan and place it in the oven until the butter melts. Then, with a piece of crumpled plastic wrap, spread the butter all over. Place the pan in the freezer (preferably) or the refrigerator (a cold pan will make it easier to spread the dough).

Shake the peanuts lightly in a large strainer to remove some of the excess salt. Then place them in the bowl of a food processor fitted with the metal chopping blade and pulse the machine seven times. Some of the nuts will be fine, and some will still be whole. Remove the nuts from the processor and set aside.

Sift together the flour, salt, baking soda, and cinnamon; set aside.

In the small bowl of an electric mixer beat the butter until soft. Beat in the vanilla and then the sugar.

In a small bowl beat the egg lightly, only until mixed but not until foamy.

Add 2 tablespoons of the egg (reserve the remaining egg) to the butter and sugar mixture, beat to mix, and then add the sifted dry ingredients and beat on low speed only until mixed.

Remove the bowl from the mixer. Stir in half the chopped peanuts (reserve remaining peanuts).

Now, this next step needs patience. First place the dough by small (really small) spoonfuls all over the pan. And then, with well-floured fingertips, spread the dough all over. It will be a very, very thin layer, and it will be necessary to reflour your fingertips very often. You will think that there is not enough dough. But there is, just barely.

Brush off any loose flour remaining on top of the dough.

Pour the reserved beaten egg all over the dough and, with the palm of your hand and your fingertips, spread the egg over all.

Finally sprinkle the reserved chopped nuts over all.

Cover with a piece of baking parchment, wax paper, or plastic wrap, and press firmly all over with the palms of both hands to be sure there are no loose nuts. It's a good idea to also use something flat (a cookie sheet or a telephone book) and press that over all to level the dough. Then remove the parchment, paper, or plastic.

Bake for 25 to 27 minutes, until the top is beautifully browned.

Remove from the oven and let stand until cool.

Cover the cooled pan with a cookie sheet and turn the pan and sheet upside down. Remove the pan and carefully peel away the foil. Cover with another cookie sheet and turn upside down again, leaving the cake right side up.

With a long, firm, sharp knife cut the cake into quarters. Then cut each quarter into 4 large, or 8 smaller, bars. (If you wish, you can still cut each bar in half again, making really small, bite-sized bars that are lovely.)

These must be stored airtight. Either place them in a covered freezer box or wrap them individually in clear cellophane or wax paper.

Palm Springs Lemon Squares with Dates

The date trees in and around Palm Springs, California, are spectacular—and the dates are delicious. People there use dates in everything, especially in shakes (a milk shake made in a blender with ice cream and dates). In these lemon squares they put a layer of sliced dates between the crisp brown sugar shortbread on the bottom and the sour lemon custardy topping. The combination is great—these are fabulous.

You will need Pam or some other non-stick spray.

16 SQUARES

SHORTBREAD CRUST
1 cup plus 3 tablespoons sifted unbleached flour
Pinch of salt
¼ firmly packed cup light brown sugar
4 ounces (1 stick) unsalted butter

Adjust a rack to the center of the oven and preheat oven to 350 degrees. You will need an 8-inch-square baking pan. Turn the pan upside down on the work surface. Center a 12-inch square of aluminum foil, shiny side down, over the pan. Press down on the sides and corners with your hands to shape the foil to the pan. Remove the foil. Run some tap water into the pan to wet it all over (the wet pan helps to hold the foil in place). Pour out all but about a tablespoon of the water. Place the foil in the pan and press it against the bottom and sides. Press on the foil in the corners to make it as smooth as possible. Place a piece of butter (additional to that called for in ingredients) in the pan, put it in the oven to melt, and then, with a piece of crumpled plastic wrap spread the butter all over the bottom and sides. Place the pan in the freezer (preferably) or refrigerator (a cold pan makes it easier to shape the bottom crust).

Place the flour, salt, and sugar in the bowl of a food processor fitted with the metal chopping blade. Pulse a few times to mix. Cut the butter into about six pieces and add to the processor bowl. Process about 30 seconds, until the ingredients hold together.

Remove the blade and turn the ingredients out of the bowl.

Remove the pan from the freezer. Put some flour in the pan, shake the pan to coat it all over, then tap it over paper to remove excess.

Hold the mound of dough in one hand, and with the other hand break off small pieces (each about a rounded teaspoonful) and place them all over the bottom of the pan.

Flour your fingertips and press the dough all over the bottom; reflour your fingertips as necessary.

Bake for 25 minutes, until lightly browned.

While the crust is baking, prepare the Lemon Topping.

LEMON TOPPING

4 ounces (1 loosely packed cup) pitted dates
1/4 cup plus 1 teaspoon sifted unbleached flour
1/2 teaspoon baking powder
1/8 teaspoon salt
2 eggs graded "large"
1 cup granulated sugar
1/3 cup fresh lemon juice (Grate the rinds to use before squeezing the
    juice.)
Finely grated rind of 2 cold and firm lemons
Confectioners sugar (to sprinkle on before serving)

With scissors, cut each date into three pieces and set aside.

Sift together the flour, baking powder, and salt.

In a small bowl beat the eggs with the sugar, lemon juice, and the sifted dry ingredients until well mixed.

Stir in the grated rind.

When the crust is baked, remove it from the oven and reduce oven temperature to 325 degrees.

Thoroughly spray the sides and corners of the pan containing the crust with Pam or some other nonstick spray. (Even though the sides are buttered and floured, for this recipe they should also be sprayed or the cake will stick.)

Place the dates all over the crust. Pour the lemon mixture all over the dates and crust. With a fingertip, press down gently on the dates just to wet the tops.

Bake for 35 minutes. The top will look pale and will feel a little crusty.

Remove the pan from the oven; let stand until cool.

Cover the pan with a small cutting board, cookie sheet, or what have you. Turn the pan and board or sheet upside down. Remove the pan. Gently, carefully, and slowly peel off the foil (being very cautious around the sides).

Cover the bottom of the cake with a piece of baking parchment or wax paper and another small board or cookie sheet. Turn upside down again, leaving the cake right side up.

Place in the freezer for an hour or more. (This cuts best when it is frozen.)

With a long, firm, sharp knife, cut the cake into quarters and then cut each quarter into four squares.

Sprinkle confectioners sugar generously through a fine strainer over the squares.

These can be served frozen, or cold from the refrigerator. I have stored them in the freezer for days and served them really frozen. I cut each square into two thin slices just before serving.

Penuche Pecan Bars

32 BARS

Unusually chewy bars loaded with pecans. I have no idea what makes them so deliciously moist and chewy. Maybe the texture is the result of cooking the sugar and eggs together before mixing them with the other ingredients.

These contain no butter or oil, and are even better the second day, so plan ahead. (By the way, penuche is the name of a brown sugar fudge.)

4 eggs graded "large"
1 pound (2½ packed cups) light brown sugar
1¾ cups sifted unbleached flour
1 teaspoon baking powder
¼ teaspoon salt
1 pound (4½ cups) pecan halves
1½ teaspoons vanilla extract

Adjust a rack to the center of the oven and preheat the oven to 350 degrees. Prepare a 9 by 13 by 2-inch pan as follows: Turn the pan upside down on the work surface. Center a 16-inch length of aluminum foil, shiny side down, over the pan. Press on the sides and corners to shape the foil to the pan, then remove the foil. Turn the pan right side up. Run some tap water into the pan, then pour out all but 1 or 2 tablespoons (the water in the pan helps to hold the foil in place). Place the foil in the pan and press gently all over to shape it to the pan. To butter the pan place a piece of butter in the pan and place the pan in the oven to melt the butter. Spread the melted butter with a piece of crumpled plastic wrap; set the pan aside.

In the top part of a large double boiler beat the eggs lightly just to mix. Stir in the sugar—if there are lumps in the sugar just press on them with a rubber spatula (preferably a large one) to break them up. Place over hot water in the bottom part of the double boiler on moderate heat. Cook for 20 minutes, stirring frequently and scraping the sides with a rubber spatula.

Sift together the flour, baking powder, and salt; set aside.

Place the pecans in a large mixing bowl.

After 20 minutes of cooking the eggs and sugar, stir in the vanilla, then pour the mixture over the nuts. Stir to mix. Add the sifted dry ingredients and stir to mix again.

Turn the hot mixture into the prepared pan. Spread smooth.

Bake for about 25 minutes, or until a toothpick gently inserted in the middle comes out slightly wet, almost but not completely dry.

Let stand until cool.

Then cover the pan with a cookie sheet or a rack, turn upside down, remove the pan and peel off the foil, cover with a length of wax paper or baking pan liner paper and then another rack or cookie sheet and turn upside down again, leaving the cake right side up.

Refrigerate for an hour, or overnight if you wish. Place the cold cake on a cutting board. Use a serrated French bread knife to cut the cake into bars. First cut it into quarters, then cut each quarter into 8 pieces.

The pieces can be individually wrapped in clear cellophane, wax paper, or aluminum foil, or they can be put in an airtight plastic box with wax paper between the layers.

These might seem a little too sticky (yummy) when you cut them, but after standing a few hours they will be just right. If just the bottoms feel sticky, let them stand upside down; they will dry rather quickly.

Napa Valley Almond Bars

Thin bar cookies loaded with chopped almonds and covered with chocolate and more chopped almonds. They are extremely crisp and crunchy, very pretty, and positively delicious. The recipe comes from a California chef who often makes them to serve with fruit and ice cream.

32 BARS

10 ounces (2 cups) blanched (skinned) almonds
8 ounces (2 sticks) unsalted butter
1 teaspoon vanilla extract
¼ teaspoon salt
½ packed cup light brown sugar
½ cup granulated sugar
1 egg yolk
1¾ cups sifted unbleached flour
6 ounces (1 cup) semisweet chocolate morsels

Adjust a rack one-third up from the bottom of the oven and preheat oven to 350 degrees. Prepare a 13 by 9½ by 2-inch pan as follows: Turn the pan upside down. Center a 17-inch length of aluminum foil over the pan, shiny side down. Press down on the sides and corners to shape the foil to fit the pan. Remove the foil. Run some tap water into the pan to wet it all over. Pour out all but about 2 tablespoons of water (the wet pan helps to hold the foil in place). Place the shaped foil in the pan and press gently all over to fit it to the pan. To butter the pan, place a piece of butter (additional to that in the ingredients) in the pan and place it in the oven until the butter melts. With a pastry brush or a piece of crumpled plastic wrap, spread the butter all over the bottom and sides. Pour some fine dry bread crumbs (I use bought, unflavored crumbs) in the pan, and over a large piece of paper tilt the pan in all directions to spread the crumbs all over. Turn the pan upside down to allow excess crumbs to fall out. Place the pan in the freezer or refrigerator (a cold pan will make it easier to spread the dough).

To toast the almonds, place them in a shallow pan in the 350-degree oven for about 10 or 12 minutes, shaking or stirring occasionally, until the nuts are just barely colored and smell great. Let cool.

Chop the nuts by placing them in the bowl of a food processor fitted with the metal chopping blade. Pulse the machine seven or eight times. Some of the nuts will be powdery, some will be in pieces, and a few will still be whole, but if you process them any longer they will all be too fine. Set aside.

In the large bowl of an electric mixer beat the butter until soft. Add the vanilla and both sugars and beat until well mixed. Beat in the egg yolk, then the sifted flour. Finally, beat in 1 cup of the chopped nuts (reserve remaining 1 cup nuts).

Place the dough by rounded tablespoonfuls all over the bottom of the cold pan.

Dip your fingers in flour and start to press the dough into an even layer. Continue to dip your fingers in flour each time, and press the dough all over to make an even layer.

Bake for 33 minutes, reversing the pan front to back once during baking. When done, the layer should be a rich golden color and it should just start to come away from the sides of the pan.

Remove from the oven and without waiting, sprinkle the chocolate evenly all over the layer. Return the pan to the oven for about 2 minutes, until the chocolate is soft enough to be spread. With the underside of a tablespoon, spread the chocolate all over and then, without waiting, sprinkle the reserved nuts evenly all over.

Cover the nuts with a length of plastic wrap and press down all over with your hands to press the nuts securely into the chocolate. Remove the plastic wrap and let the cake stand for several hours, until the chocolate is firm. If necessary, place the pan in the refrigerator or freezer for a few minutes.

You are going to turn the whole thing upside down. In order to prevent loose nuts from flying around, cover the pan with a length of aluminum foil and press the foil firmly around the sides of the pan. Cover with a cookie sheet. Turn upside down. Remove the pan and the foil lining. Cover with another cookie sheet and turn upside down again, leaving the cake right side up. Remove the aluminum foil covering.

With a long and sharp knife cut the cake into quarters, then cut each quarter into 8 bars.

If the chocolate has softened again, just let the bars stand, uncovered, at room temperature until the chocolate becomes firm.

Wrap the bars individually in clear cellophane, wax paper, or foil, or place them in an airtight box with wax paper between the layers.

Coconut and Walnut Oatmeal Bars

32 BARS

Deliciously chewy, oatmeal bars. Mildly spiced. Easy to make. These are great anytime, but are especially appreciated at a picnic. They travel well and they mail well.

7 ounces (2 cups) walnuts
1 cup sifted flour
Scant $^1/_4$ teaspoon salt
Scant $^1/_4$ teaspoon ground nutmeg
    (Nutmeg is strong; measure care-
    fully—a bit less is better than a bit
    more.)
Scant $^1/_4$ teaspoon ground allspice
$^1/_2$ teaspoon ground ginger
2 cups quick-cooking (not "instant") oat-
    meal
$3^1/_2$ ounces (1 packed cup) shredded
    coconut
7 ounces ($1^3/_4$ sticks) unsalted butter
2 tablespoons honey
$^2/_3$ firmly packed cup light brown sugar
1 teaspoon baking soda
1 teaspoon vanilla extract

Adjust a rack one-third up from the bottom of the oven and preheat oven to 275 degrees. Line a 9 by 13 by 2-inch pan with aluminum foil as follows: Turn the pan upside down. Center a 17-inch length of foil, shiny side down, over the pan. With your hands, press down on the sides and corners of the foil to shape it to the pan. Remove the foil. Turn the pan right side up. Place the shaped foil in the pan and press gently all over to fit it to the pan. To butter the pan, place a piece of butter (additional to that called for in ingredients) in the pan and place it in the oven until the butter melts. With a brush or with a piece of crumpled plastic wrap spread the butter all over the foil. Place the pan in the freezer (preferably) or refrigerator (a cold pan will make it easier to spread the dough).

Break the walnuts into large pieces; set aside.

Sift together into a large mixing bowl the flour, salt, nutmeg, allspice, and ginger. Add the oatmeal, coconut, and walnuts and stir with a wooden spatula or wooden spoon to mix.

Place the butter in a medium-sized saucepan over moderate heat until melted. Add the honey to the butter (if you dip the measuring spoon in the butter before measuring the honey, the honey won't stick to the spoon). Add the sugar and stir over heat briefly to partially melt the sugar. Remove from the heat. Stir in the baking soda and the vanilla.

Add the butter mixture to the dry ingredients and stir well to mix.

Turn into the prepared pan. Distribute the mixture all over the bottom of the pan. Then, press down all over with the bottom of a large spoon. Now, to make the layer of dough more compact, cover the dough with a length of plastic wrap and press all over with the bottom of a glass or measuring cup. Remove the plastic wrap.

Bake for 50 minutes, reversing the pan front to back once during baking to insure even browning. After 50 minutes the dough will be golden brown, but it will not feel done if you press on it with your fingertip. Even though it doesn't feel done, remove the pan from the oven and let stand until cooled to room temperature.

Cover with a cookie sheet or a cutting board. Turn the pan and sheet or board upside down. Remove the pan and peel off the aluminum foil. Cover with another cookie sheet or cutting board and turn upside down again, leaving the cake right side up.

The cake should be chilled before it is cut into bars. It can be done in the refrigerator or the freezer (in the freezer, 15 to 20 minutes is long enough; if you freeze it longer, it will be hard to cut).

Then, with a long and sharp knife cut the cake into quarters, and finally cut each quarter into 8 bars.

The cookies can be stored in a plastic freezer box (or any other airtight box), or they can be wrapped individually in clear cellophane, wax paper, or aluminum foil.

Chocolate on Oatmeal Bars

24 TO 32 SMALL BARS

There is a crisp oatmeal layer on the bottom, and a moist and soft chocolate and walnut layer on the top. You will need Pam or some other nonstick spray.

OATMEAL LAYER

3 ounces (¾ stick) unsalted butter
½ firmly packed cup light brown sugar
½ cup sifted unbleached flour
⅛ teaspoon salt
¼ teaspoon baking soda
1 cup old-fashioned (not "instant") oatmeal

Adjust a rack one-third up from the bottom of the oven and preheat oven to 350 degrees. Prepare a 9-inch-square pan as follows: Turn the pan upside down. Center a 12-inch square of aluminum foil, shiny side down, over the pan. Press down on the sides and corners to shape the foil to fit the pan. Remove the foil. Place the shaped foil in the pan and press gently all over to fit it to the pan. With your thumb, smooth the corners to flatten the wrinkles. Spray the pan all over with Pam or some other nonstick spray. Set aside.

Place the butter in a small saucepan over moderate heat. When melted, add the brown sugar and cook for 30 seconds. Set aside.

Sift together the flour, salt, and baking soda. Place in a large bowl and stir in the oatmeal. Then add the butter mixture and stir to mix.

Turn into the prepared pan, and with floured fingertips, press the dough evenly all over the bottom of the pan.

Bake for 10 minutes, until golden colored.

Meanwhile, prepare the chocolate layer.

CHOCOLATE LAYER

3 ounces milk chocolate
⅔ cup minus 2 tablespoons sifted unbleached flour
2 tablespoons unsweetened cocoa powder
¼ teaspoon baking powder

⅛ teaspoon salt
2½ ounces (¾ cup) walnuts
½ teaspoon vanilla extract
¼ cup milk
2 ounces (½ stick) unsalted butter
1 ounce unsweetened chocolate
¾ cup granulated sugar
1 egg graded "large"

Cut the milk chocolate into ¼-inch pieces; set aside.

Sift together the flour, cocoa, baking powder, and salt; set aside.

Break or cut the walnuts into medium-sized pieces; set aside.

Stir the vanilla into the milk; set aside.

In a small double boiler over hot water on moderate heat—or in a small, heavy saucepan over low heat—melt the butter and unsweetened chocolate. Stir to mix, then transfer to the small bowl of an electric mixer. Beat in the sugar and the egg. On low speed beat in half the sifted dry ingredients, then the milk, and finally the remaining dry ingredients.

Remove the bowl from the mixer and stir in the walnuts.

As soon as the oatmeal layer is baked, remove the pan from the oven and sprinkle the chopped milk chocolate all over the hot oatmeal layer.

Pour the chocolate mixture on top and spread it to make an even layer.

Bake for about 30 minutes, until a toothpick gently inserted in the middle comes out with just a bit of the chocolate mixture clinging to it.

Let stand until cool.

Cover with a board or a cookie sheet. Turn upside down. Remove the pan and the foil. Cover with another board or sheet and turn upside down again, leaving the cake right side up.

To cut, use a long, thin, sharp knife and cut the cake into quarters. Cut each piece in half, making 2 strips, then cut each strip into 3 or 4 bars.

Store in an airtight container with wax paper between the layers or wrap individually in clear cellophane or wax paper.

Bittersweet Chocolate Brownies

16 BROWNIES

Standard recipes for this volume of brownies use 1½ or 2 ounces of chocolate. This one uses 8 ounces, is flavored with espresso, and has an enormous amount of walnuts— a delicious combination. Finally, when this cake pan is removed from the oven, a bit of dark rum is sprinkled or brushed on top. You can also use cognac, scotch, or bourbon, or you can leave it plain.

You need an 8 by 8 by 2-inch pan.

2 ounces unsweetened chocolate
6 ounces semisweet chocolate
2 tablespoons unsalted butter
7 ounces (2 cups) walnuts
½ cup sifted unbleached flour
¼ teaspoon baking powder
¼ teaspoon salt
2 eggs graded "large"
¾ cup granulated sugar
½ teaspoon vanilla extract
2 teaspoons dry powdered instant espresso (I use Medaglia D'Oro.)
3 tablespoons dark rum, cognac, scotch, or bourbon

Adjust a rack one-third up from the bottom of the oven and preheat oven to 350 degrees. Prepare an 8 by 8 by 2-inch pan as follows: Turn the pan upside down. Center a 12-inch length of aluminum foil, shiny side down, over the pan. Press down on the sides and corners to shape the foil to fit the pan. Remove the foil. Run some tap water into the pan to wet it all over. Pour out all but about a tablespoon of the water (the wet pan helps to hold the foil in place). Place the shaped foil in the pan and press gently all over to fit the foil to the pan. To butter the pan, place a piece of butter (additional to that in the ingredients) in the pan and place it in the oven to melt. With a piece of crumpled plastic wrap, spread the butter all over the bottom and sides. Place the pan in the freezer or refrigerator (a cold pan will make it easier to spread the thick batter).

In the top of a small double boiler over shallow hot water on moderate heat melt the chocolates together with the butter. Stir to mix, then remove the top of the double boiler and set aside.

Break the walnuts into medium-sized pieces; set aside.

Sift together the flour, baking powder, and salt; set aside.

In the small bowl of an electric mixer beat the eggs, sugar, vanilla, and espresso on high speed for about a minute. Add the melted chocolate mixture (which may still be warm) and beat just to mix. Then add the sifted dry ingredients and beat on low speed only until mixed.

Remove the bowl from the mixer. Add the nuts and stir to mix. It will be a very thick and stiff mixture.

Turn the mixture into the prepared pan. Smooth the top with the bottom of a spoon.

Bake for 40 minutes. When done, a toothpick gently inserted in the middle will come out with a bit of chocolate clinging to it. If you insert the toothpick near the edge, it should come out almost clean.

As soon as you remove the pan from the oven, brush or drizzle the rum, cognac, scotch, or bourbon all over the top. (The top of the cake will dry as it cools.)

Let stand until cool.

Cover the pan with a small board or cookie sheet and turn the pan and board or cookie sheet upside down. Remove the pan and the foil lining. Cover the cake with another small board or sheet and turn upside down again, leaving the cake right side up.

It is best to chill the cake before you cut it, either in the refrigerator for a few hours or in the freezer for about an hour.

Then with a sharp, heavy knife with a long blade, cut the cake into quarters, and cut each piece into 4 brownies.

If you wish, wrap these individually in clear cellophane, wax paper, or aluminum foil, or just place them in an airtight container.

I store these in the refrigerator and serve them cold, but they can be served at room temperature if you wish.

Jane Freiman's Brownies

16 BROWNIES

I thought I had made—or at least read—every recipe in existence for brownies. But I recently reread a delicious book, *Dinner Party*, by my friend Jane Freiman, and I came across this recipe, which is very new to me. The procedure is radically different from others. And the temperature is different. And these have sour cream. And, although I thought I had pushed chocolate to the outer limits of chocolatedom, these have even more chocolate. This brownie is what brownies are all about—dark, thick, moist, chewy, and dense. Not cakelike. If you serve these at room temperature, they are fragile and moist; if you serve them refrigerated, they are more firm and more like fudge candy. Either way, you can't go wrong.

Incidentally, you can store these in the freezer and serve them directly from the freezer without thawing. They do not get too hard. Cut each frozen brownie into two narrow brownies and serve immediately. Sensational.

¼ *cup sifted unbleached flour*
¼ *teaspoon baking powder*
¼ *teaspoon salt*
8 ounces semisweet or bittersweet chocolate
5 ounces (1¼ cups) walnuts
2 eggs graded "large"
2 teaspoons vanilla
⅓ *cup sour cream*
4 ounces (1 stick) unsalted butter
¾ *cup granulated sugar*

Adjust a rack to the center of the oven and preheat oven to 300 degrees. Prepare an 8 by 8 by 2-inch pan as follows: Turn the pan upside down. Center a 12-inch length of aluminum foil, shiny side down, over the pan. Press down on the sides and corners to shape the foil to fit the pan. Remove the foil. Place the shaped foil in the pan and press gently all over to fit it to the pan. With crumpled plastic wrap, spread room-temperature butter all over the bottom and sides. Then pour some fine dry bread crumbs (I use bought, unflavored crumbs) into the pan and—over a large piece of paper—tilt the pan in all directions to crumb it all over, then turn the pan upside down to shake out excess. Set the prepared pan aside.

Sift together the flour, baking powder, and salt; set aside.

Chop or break the chocolate into small pieces; set aside.

Cut or break the walnuts into medium-sized pieces; set aside.

In a small bowl beat the eggs, vanilla, and sour cream just to mix; set aside.

In a saucepan with at least a 1-quart capacity, over moderate heat, melt the butter. Add the sugar and stir for a minute or so until the sugar is partially melted. Then add the chocolate and stir until melted.

Transfer to a large mixing bowl. Stir in the egg mixture, then the sifted dry ingredients. If the mixture is not perfectly smooth, beat it briefly with an electric mixer or a manual beater. Stir in the nuts.

Pour into the baking pan and smooth the top.

Bake for about 1 hour, until a toothpick gently inserted in the middle comes out almost—but not completely—clean.

Let stand at room temperature until completely cool.

Then cover the pan with a small sheet or board. Turn upside down. Remove the pan and the foil. Cover with a piece of wax paper and another small sheet or board. Turn upside down again, leaving the cake right side up.

Chill the cake before cutting it; it will be easy to cut neat squares if the cake is cold enough. Place it in the freezer for about an hour or longer, or in the refrigerator for at least several hours.

With a long, thin, sharp knife, carefully cut the cake into quarters, then cut each quarter into 4 brownies.

You can either wrap these individually in clear cellophane, wax paper, or aluminum foil, or you can place them in an airtight box.

Heath Bar Brownies

24 SMALL BROWNIES

In the immortal words of Mae West, "Too much of a good thing is wonderful." The Heath bars—a lot of them—are cut up and mixed into the brownie mixture and are also sprinkled on top. These are intensely chocolate. And sexy.

2½ ounces (¾ cup) pecan halves or pieces
6¼ ounces Heath bars (see Note)
2 ounces unsweetened chocolate
4 ounces (1 stick) unsalted butter
2 eggs graded "large"
½ teaspoon vanilla extract
¼ teaspoon salt
¾ cup granulated sugar
1 cup sifted unbleached flour

Adjust a rack one-third up from the bottom of the oven and preheat oven to 350 degrees. Prepare an 8-inch-square pan as follows: Turn the pan upside down, center a 12-inch square of aluminum foil, shiny side down, over the pan. Press down on the sides and corners of the foil to shape it to the pan. Remove the foil. Turn the pan right side up, place the foil in the pan, and press all over to fit it to the pan. To butter the foil, place a piece of butter (additional to that in ingredients) in the pan and place it in the oven to melt. Then, with crumpled plastic wrap, spread the butter all over. Set the pan aside.

Toast the pecans in a shallow pan in the oven for about 12 minutes, until they are very hot and smell toasted. Set aside.

To cut up the Heath bars, work on a cutting board with a sharp and heavy knife. Cut through the long sides into slices ¼ to ⅓ inch wide (you will have about 1½ cups of cut-up Heath bars). Chop a scant ¼ cup of the cut-up bars into smaller pieces (to sprinkle on top); keep these separate.

Place the unsweetened chocolate and butter in the top of a small double boiler over warm water on moderate heat. Stir occasionally until melted. Remove the top of the double boiler and set aside.

In the small bowl of an electric mixer beat the eggs, vanilla, salt, and sugar until mixed. Add the melted chocolate mixture (which may still be warm) and beat only to mix. Then add the flour and beat only to mix. Remove the bowl from the mixer.

Stir in the nuts and all but the ¼ cup of smaller Heath bar pieces.

Turn into the prepared pan and spread smooth. Sprinkle the smaller pieces of Heath bars over the top.

Bake for 28 minutes, until a toothpick inserted in the middle comes out just barely clean.

Remove the pan from the oven; let stand until cool.

Cover with a small cutting board or cookie sheet and turn upside down; remove the pan and peel away the foil. Cover the cake with a piece of baking parchment or wax paper and another board or sheet, and turn upside down again, leaving the cake right side up.

Refrigerate for about an hour.

Then, with a long, thin, sharp knife, cut the cake into quarters, cutting with a back-and-forth sawing motion. Cut each quarter in half, then cut each strip into 3 small bars.

Place in an airtight container with wax paper between the layers, or wrap individually in clear cellophane or wax paper.

These can be served at room temperature or refrigerated—I like them best cold.

Note: Heath bars come in different sizes. You can use either the bars that are packaged two in a package and are labeled 1.4 ounces per package (you will want 5 packages). Or you can use the miniatures ("snack bars") that come in a bag labeled 9 ounces (you will want 20 of these miniatures).

Palm Beach Brownies with Chocolate-Covered Mints

At a party that Mr. and Mrs. David Brinkley gave in Miami Beach I was introduced to Mrs. Tip O'Neill. She heard my name and without hesitation she said, "Palm Beach Brownies." This has happened to me many times. The recipe for Palm Beach Brownies is one of the two or three most popular recipes in all of my books.

The original recipe is in my chocolate book, with this introduction: "The biggest, thickest, gooiest, chewiest, darkest, sweetest, mostest-of-the-most . . . with an almost wet middle and a crisp-crunchy top." This recipe is the same as the original, but I have added a layer of chocolate-covered mints in the middle. The mints stay whole (they don't melt), and they look and taste gorgeous.

The baked cake should be refrigerated for at least a few hours, or overnight, or frozen for an hour or two before it is cut into bars.

32 JUMBO BROWNIES—
ACTUALLY 6½ POUNDS
OF BROWNIES

8 ounces unsweetened chocolate
8 ounces (2 sticks) unsalted butter
8 ounces (2 generous cups) walnuts
5 eggs graded "large"
2 teaspoons vanilla extract
½ teaspoon almond extract
¼ teaspoon salt
1 tablespoon plus 1 teaspoon powdered instant espresso (I use
    Medaglia D'Oro from an Italian grocery store.)
3¾ cups granulated sugar
1⅔ cups sifted unbleached flour
Two 14- or 15.4-ounce bags York chocolate-covered peppermint
    patties, unwrapped

Adjust an oven rack one-third up from the bottom and preheat oven to 425 degrees. Line a 9 by 13 by 2-inch pan as follows: Invert the pan and center a 17-inch length of aluminum foil, shiny side down, over the pan. (If you are using a Magic Line® pan that has straight sides and square corners, use heavy-duty foil or the sharp corners will tear it. This is a wonderful pan and makes beautiful brownies.) With your hands, press down on the sides and corners of the foil to shape it to the pan. Remove the foil. Turn the pan right side up. Place the foil in the pan and very carefully press it into place in the pan. Now, to butter the foil, place a piece of butter (additional to that in ingredients) in the pan, and put the pan in the oven. When the butter is melted use a pastry brush or a piece of crumpled plastic wrap to spread the butter all over the foil. Set the prepared pan aside.

Place the chocolate and the butter in the top of a large double boiler over hot water on moderate heat, or in a 4- to 6-cup heavy saucepan over low heat. Stir occasionally, until the chocolate and butter are melted. Stir to mix. Remove from the heat and set aside.

Break the walnuts into large pieces; set aside.

In the large bowl of an electric mixer beat the eggs with the vanilla and almond extracts, salt, espresso, and sugar at high speed for 10 minutes. On low speed add the chocolate mixture (which may still be warm) and beat only until mixed. Then add the flour and again beat on low speed only until mixed. Remove the bowl from the mixer.

Stir in the nuts.

Pour half the mixture (about 3½ cups) into the prepared pan and smooth the top.

Place a layer of the mints, touching each other and the edges of the pan, all over the chocolate layer. Cut some mints to fill in large spaces on the edges. (You will not use all the mints. There will be some left over.)

Pour the remaining chocolate mixture all over the pan and smooth the top.

Bake for 35 minutes reversing the pan front to back once during baking to insure even baking. At the end of 35 minutes the cake will have a firm crust on top, but if you insert a toothpick in the middle it will come out wet and covered with chocolate. Nevertheless, it is done. Do not bake any longer.

Remove the pan from the oven; let stand until cool. Cover the pan with a cookie sheet and invert the pan and the sheet. Remove the pan and the foil lining. Cover the cake with a length of wax paper and another cookie sheet and invert again, leaving the cake right side up.

Now the cake must be refrigerated for a few hours or overnight before it is cut into bars.

When you are ready to cut the cake, use a long, heavy knife with a sharp blade, either serrated or straight—try both. Cut the cake into quarters. Cut each quarter in half, cutting through the long sides. Finally, cut each piece into 4 bars, cutting through the long sides. (I think these are better in narrow bar shapes than in squares.)

Pack in an airtight box, or wrap individually in clear cellophane, wax paper, or foil.

These freeze perfectly and can be served very cold or at room temperature.

Notes: When you remove the cake from the pan you might see burned edges. (You might not—it depends on the pan.) If you do, you can leave them on or cut them off. I cut them off, but I have friends who say that this is the best part.

These are huge! For some occasions you might want to cut them smaller. They are equally delicious, and sometimes they seem more appropriate.

P.S. Once upon a time . . . I was in the cookie business. I made the original Palm Beach Brownies (without the mints) and sold them to the Jordan Marsh department store here in Miami. I wrapped them individually in clear cellophane and then packaged them in white boxes with clear plastic tops. I wrote the recipe by hand and had it xeroxed. Each box contained a dozen brownies and the recipe. Business was great, but it took up almost all my time. When I started writing cookbooks, I had to quit the brownie business. But it was wonderful while it lasted.

Variation

Recently, I was invited to bake cookies for an event held by the American Institute of Wine and Food. It was a South Sea Islands dinner held at The Kampong in Coconut Grove, Florida. The Kampong is the former home of Dr. David Fairchild, botanist, horticulturist and America's foremost plant collector. He named his home after the many kampongs he visited throughout South Asia.

I made up these Bali Hai Brownies. I used the above recipe without the walnuts and the mints. I added the following ingredients, just stirred into the dough:

6 ounces crystalized ginger, cut into ¼- to ½-inch pieces
10 ounces (about 3 packed cups) shredded coconut
10 ounces (2 generous cups) whole macadamia nuts (I use the
*   Mauna Loa nuts that come in a jar—they are roasted and*
*   salted.)*

The brownies were lush, moist (like thick macaroons), exotic, and dramatic (the whole macadamias were startling). The recipe is extravagant—the ingredients are expensive. The brownies are extraordinary.

The ginger is optional. The flavor is delicious, but the brownies are equally fabulous with or without it.

Skinny Peanut Bars

Extra-thin bars that are crisp on top, but soft, chewy, yummy caramel-like below. They are plain—and delicious—they taste like they are made with peanut butter, but they're not.

32 BARS

8 ounces (2 cups) salted peanuts
2 tablespoons unbleached flour
1 teaspoon baking powder
2 eggs graded "large"
1 packed cup light brown sugar
1 teaspoon vanilla extract

Adjust a rack to the middle of the oven and preheat oven to 325 degrees. Prepare a 10 by 15 by 1-inch jelly roll pan as follows: Turn the pan upside down. Cut a piece of aluminum foil 17 inches long. Center the foil, shiny side down, over the pan, and with your hands, press down on the sides and corners to shape the foil. Remove the foil. Run some tap water into the pan. Pour out all but about 2 tablespoons (the wet pan helps to hold the foil in place). Then place the foil in the pan and press it firmly against the bottom and sides.

To butter the pan, place a piece of butter in the pan and place the pan in the oven until the butter melts. With a piece of crumpled plastic wrap spread the butter all over the bottom and sides and then place the pan in the freezer or refrigerator (it is easier to spread the thin layer of dough if the pan is very cold).

Place the peanuts, flour, and baking powder in the bowl of a food processor fitted with the metal chopping blade. Process about 15 seconds, until the nuts are in tiny pieces. Turn into a large mixing bowl and set aside.

In the small bowl of an electric mixer beat the eggs with the sugar and vanilla at high speed for about 5 minutes, until the mixture is pale and forms a ribbon when the beaters are raised.

Pour the egg mixture over the nut mixture and, with a rubber spatula, stir/fold together until mixed.

Turn into the cold pan, and with the bottom of a large spoon spread level.

Bake about 23 minutes, reversing the pan front to back once during baking. (Do not overbake.) When done, there will be a thin crust on top. It will be only lightly colored.

Remove from the oven and let stand at room temperature until completely cool.

Cover the pan with a cookie sheet or anything else flat and large enough. Turn upside down. Remove the pan. Now, gently peel off the foil. Cover the cake with another cookie sheet (or something else) and turn upside down again, leaving the cake right side up.

With a long, sharp knife, cut the cake into quarters, then cut each quarter into 8 bars. If the edges are so dry and crisp that they crumble, trim them.

These can be wrapped two together (bottoms together) in clear cellophane, wax paper, or foil, or they can be packed in a Rubbermaid box. (In a box they should be placed flat, bottoms down.)

Variation

In the nothing-succeeds-like-excess department, Milk Chocolate Chip: Stir in 1 cup milk chocolate morsels just before turning the mixture into the pan.

If you wish, sandwich two baked bars (either plain or chocolate chip) together with a moderately thin layer of peanut butter in the middle. Charlie Brown never had it so good.

Chocolate Chip Peanut Butter Bars

32 BARS

Moist and yummy peanut butter bars loaded with chocolate chips and peanuts. My friends say "love 'em, love 'em, love 'em."

4 ounces (1 cup) salted peanuts
½ cup granulated sugar
1 cup sifted unbleached flour
1 teaspoon baking powder
⅛ teaspoon salt
3 ounces (¾ stick) unsalted butter
1 teaspoon vanilla extract
1 tablespoon any jam, jelly, or marmalade
½ cup smooth or chunky peanut butter
¾ packed cup light or dark brown sugar
2 eggs graded "large"
12 ounces (2 cups) milk chocolate
  morsels

Adjust a rack to the center of the oven and preheat oven to 350 degrees. Line a 9 by 13 by 2-inch pan as follows: Place the pan upside down. Center a 17-inch length of aluminum foil, shiny side down, over the pan. With your hands, press down on the sides and corners of the pan to shape the foil to fit. Remove the foil. Run tap water into the pan, pour out all but 1 or 2 tablespoons (the wet pan helps hold the foil in place), and place the shaped foil in the pan. To butter the pan, place a piece of butter in the pan, place the pan in the oven to melt the butter, and then spread it all over with a piece of crumpled plastic wrap. Set aside.

Place the peanuts and granulated sugar in the bowl of a food processor fitted with the metal chopping blade. Pulse the machine several times to chop the peanuts a bit. Set aside.

Sift together the flour, baking powder, and salt; set aside.

In the large bowl of an electric mixer beat the butter, vanilla, and jam, jelly, or marmalade to mix. Add the peanut butter and beat to mix. Then beat in the brown sugar. Add the eggs and beat until smooth. On low speed beat in the sifted dry ingredients.

Remove the bowl from the mixer and stir in the chopped peanuts and granulated sugar. Stir in the chocolate morsels.

Turn the mixture into the prepared pan. Smooth the top.

Bake for about 35 minutes, reversing the pan front to back once during baking, until a toothpick gently inserted in the middle comes out clean.

Remove from the oven and let stand until cool.

Cover with a cookie sheet or a cutting board, turn upside down, remove the pan and foil, cover with another cookie sheet or cutting board and turn upside down again, leaving the cake right side up.

Let stand for a few hours or chill briefly until firm enough to cut.

With a long, sharp knife cut the cake into quarters. Cut each quarter in half, then cut each piece into 3 or 4 bars.

If you wish, wrap each piece in clear cellophane or wax paper, or place in an airtight box with wax paper between the layers.

SKINNY
PEANUT WAFERS

Drop
Cookies

CHOCOLATE CHIP
SOUR CREAM COOKIES

SWEET AND HOT MERINGUES

MARTHA'S VINEYARD
HERMITS

SKINNY PEANUT WAFERS

SKINNY WALNUT WAFERS

SKINNY MAPLE PECAN WAFERS

OATMEAL WAFERS

CHOCOLATI

CHOCOLATE CHIP SOUR CREAM COOKIES

SOUR CHERRY AND WALNUT CHOCOLATE HERMITS

HEATH BAR PEANUT BUTTER COOKIES

CHOCOLATE CHUNK PEANUT BUTTER COOKIES

MINT CHOCOLATE COOKIES

CHEF SUKI'S ALMOND LACE COOKIES

MARTHA'S VINEYARD HERMITS

WALNUT JUMBLES

JUMBO RAISIN AND SOUR CHERRY COOKIES

ALL-BRAN RAISIN OATMEAL COOKIES

LIGHT-AS-AIR COOKIES

SATURDAY NIGHT MERINGUES

HUNGARIAN WALNUT KISSES

SWEET AND HOT MERINGUES

Skinny Peanut Wafers

ABOUT 28 WAFERS

Five mornings a week I go to a gym and work out with a personal trainer (he's tall, dark, and handsome, and his name is Jean-Claude). Almost every afternoon—while I was writing this cookie book—I stayed home to bake cookies and write recipes. When I went to the gym the next morning, I brought the cookies I'd baked the day before. I have never made any cookies that everyone raved about with such ecstasy and abandon as all the trainers and athletes at the gym do about these Skinny Peanut Wafers. They say, "These are the best cookies in the world!" "These are the best cookies I ever ate!" (Agreed, these men might be starving for sugar. But aside from that, the cookies are truly wonderful.)

These are extremely thin wafers, crisp, crunchy, chewy, divine. They will remind you of peanut brittle. They are easy, fun, and very special. They could be served at the most elegant event, or at the simplest.

You will need Pam or some other nonstick spray.

4 ounces (1 cup) salted peanuts plus optional additional peanuts to use as topping (preferably honey roasted)
1 cup granulated sugar
2 tablespoons unsalted butter
1 cup sifted unbleached flour
1/2 teaspoon baking soda
1 egg graded "large"
2 tablespoons milk

Adjust an oven rack to the center of the oven (these will be baked only one sheet at a time). Preheat oven to 400 degrees. If you have cookie sheets with only one raised rim, these are best for this recipe; otherwise, use any cookie sheet turned upside down. Line cookie sheets with aluminum foil, shiny side up. (Do not use heavy-weight foil—the cookies won't bake well.) Set aside.

Place the 1 cup of peanuts in the bowl of a food processor fitted with a metal chopping blade. Add a few tablespoons of the sugar (reserve remaining sugar). Briefly pulse the machine 10 times to chop the nuts into coarse pieces; some will be powdery, some coarse, some still whole—OK. Set aside.

Melt the butter in a small pan over moderate heat; set aside.

Sift together the flour and baking soda; set aside.

Place the egg, milk, melted butter, and the reserved sugar in the large bowl of an electric mixer and beat until mixed. Add the sifted dry ingredients and the chopped peanuts and beat again until mixed. Transfer to a shallow bowl for ease in handling.

Rather generously spray a foil-lined sheet with Pam or some other nonstick spray.

Place the dough by slightly rounded tablespoonfuls (not heaping) on the prepared sheet, placing the mounds 3 inches apart (I place 6 on a 12 by 15½-inch sheet). Try to keep the shapes neat. Top each cookie with a few of the optional peanuts, or with as many as you can fit on the top of each cookie.

Bake one sheet at a time. After 5 minutes, reverse the sheet front to back. The cookies will rise up, spread out, and then flatten into very thin wafers with bumpy tops; they will spread out to 3½ to 4½ inches in diameter. Total baking time is 7 to 8 minutes. The cookies should bake until they are barely brown all over—but they will continue to brown a bit just from the heat of the sheet.

Remove from the oven. If the cookies have run into each other cut them apart immediately, while very hot. Cool on the sheet for a minute or two. Then slide the foil off the sheet. Let the cookies stand until they are firm enough to be removed. Then it will be easy to peel the foil away from the backs.

As soon as they are cool, store in an airtight container.

P.S. Nemo is the hottest new restaurant in Miami Beach. They recently put these cookies on their menu with my name (I gave them the recipe). They tell me that they can't make them fast enough to keep up with the demand.

Skinny Walnut Wafers

36 WAFERS

This wonderful old Southern recipe is from Charleston, South Carolina. It is quite quick and easy to mix, but you can bake only five or six at a time—one sheet at a time—and the sheet has to be lined with aluminum foil and buttered and floured each time. I tried everything, and nothing else works as well for these. But they are so good, I don't mind the buttering and flouring. The cookies are crisp and light and chewy and delicious.

8 ounces (2 1/4 cups) walnuts
5 tablespoons sifted unbleached flour
1/4 teaspoon baking powder
Pinch of salt
2 eggs graded "large"
1 teaspoon vanilla extract
1 1/4 packed cups light brown sugar

Adjust a rack to the center of the oven and preheat oven to 350 degrees. Use a flat-sided cookie sheet, or use any other sheet turned upside down. Line the sheet with aluminum foil, shiny side up. Butter the foil and dust it all over with flour. Shake and tap the sheet and foil upside down over the sink to remove excess flour. Set aside.

Break the nuts into medium-small pieces, or cut them one by one with a small, sharp knife and set aside.

Sift together the flour, baking powder, and salt; set aside.

In the small bowl of an electric mixer beat the eggs to mix. Add the vanilla and sugar and beat to mix. Then beat in the sifted dry ingredients.

Remove the bowl from the mixer and stir in the nuts.

Use a heaping teaspoonful of the batter for each cookie—they are going to spread out. On a 12 by 15 1/2-inch sheet bake only 5 cookies. On a 14 by 17-inch sheet you can bake 6 cookies.

With the tip of a fork, move the nuts around so that they are not piled on top of each other.

Bake for about 10 minutes, reversing the sheet front to back once during baking. Bake until the cookies are golden brown all over.

Remove from the oven. Slide the foil off the sheet and let stand until the cookies are slightly cool. Then pick up a corner of the foil and gently peel it away from the backs of the cookies.

Place on a rack to finish cooling.

Store in an airtight container.

Note: If these lose their crispness, reheat them for a few minutes, then cool before serving.

Skinny Maple Pecan Wafers

ABOUT 25 COOKIES

These are about as swanky and classy and pinky-in-the-airish as cookies can get, and yet they are probably the easiest cookie recipe I know. They are totally crisp and brittle and so thin you can almost see through them, like lace cookies. (I don't know any reason to do this, but you can read this recipe through the holes in the cookies.)

These are just right for a tea party or with a fruit or ice cream dessert at a luncheon or elegant dinner.

It is not necessary to use a mixer for this. It can easily be mixed in a small bowl with a rubber spatula.

$3^{1}/_{2}$ ounces (1 cup) pecan halves or pieces
$^{1}/_{2}$ cup sifted unbleached flour
$^{1}/_{4}$ teaspoon salt
$^{1}/_{8}$ teaspoon baking powder
$^{1}/_{8}$ teaspoon baking soda
2 ounces ($^{1}/_{2}$ stick) unsalted butter
$^{1}/_{2}$ cup maple syrup

Adjust a rack to the center of the oven and preheat oven to 350 degrees. Line a cookie sheet with baking parchment (preferably) or with aluminum foil, shiny side up; set aside.

Place the nuts in a shallow pan and bake for 10 minutes, until they have a strong smell of toasted nuts when you open the oven door and are very hot to the touch. Set aside to cool briefly, then break the nuts into small pieces. Set aside.

Sift together the flour, salt, baking powder, and baking soda; set aside.

In a small pan over moderate heat melt the butter.

In a small bowl mix the maple syrup with the melted butter. Add the nuts and the sifted dry ingredients and stir just to mix.

Transfer to a shallow bowl for ease in handling. (The batter will be very liquid at first, but it will thicken quickly as you work with it.)

Place the dough by rounded (not heaping) teaspoonfuls 3 inches apart on the lined sheet.

Bake one sheet at a time for 10 minutes, reversing the sheet front to back once during baking.

When done, the cookies should be colored all over, although if some of the cookies are paler in the centers they will probably finish coloring while standing on the hot sheet.

Do not underbake.

Let the baked cookies stand until they are almost or completely cool, and when they are ready it will be very easy to transfer them with a metal spatula to a rack to finish cooling, if necessary.

Repeat the directions as many times as necessary to bake the remaining batter.

When completely cool, place the cookies in an airtight container. I use a Rubbermaid freezer box.

Note: These are best when fresh, but I have served them as long as a week after making them and they were great. Just be sure they are stored in an airtight container until serving time.

Oatmeal Wafers

48 WAFERS

There's no flour in these. They are extremely crisp and crunchy, very thin, quite plain, delicious, and easy. Since they are rather small and light (not rich) they are nice to serve with a fruit or ice cream dessert, or with tea or coffee.

You will need Pam or some other nonstick spray.

2 eggs graded "large"
1 cup granulated sugar
1 tablespoon butter
1 teaspoon vanilla extract
½ teaspoon salt
2 teaspoons baking powder
2½ cups old-fashioned (not "instant") oatmeal

Adjust an oven rack to the middle of the oven and preheat oven to 375 degrees. Line cookie sheets with aluminum foil, shiny side up. (Do not use heavyweight foil—the cookies won't bake as well.)

In the small bowl of an electric mixer beat the eggs to mix. Gradually beat in the sugar. Increase the speed to high and beat for 10 minutes.

Meanwhile, in a small pan over low heat, melt the butter; set aside to cool.

Add the vanilla, salt, and baking powder to the eggs and beat to mix. Remove the bowl from the mixer. Stir in the butter.

Place the oats in a large bowl. Add the egg mixture and stir to mix. Transfer to a small bowl for ease in handling.

Spray a foil-lined sheet with Pam or some other nonstick spray.

Use a slightly rounded teaspoonful (keep these small) of the dough for each cookie. Place the mounds of dough 2½ to 3 inches apart (these spread).

Bake for about 12 minutes, reversing the sheet front to back once during baking to insure even browning. Bake until the cookies are lightly colored with paler centers. Let them cool on the sheet.

With a metal spatula, transfer the cooled cookies to paper toweling or a brown paper bag.

If you wish, the foil can be wiped and resprayed as you continue to bake the remaining cookies.

Let stand briefly and then store in an airtight container.

Chocolati

ABOUT 20 COOKIES

Delicious. Airy-light and crisp-crunchy. Plain and simple. Quick and easy. The recipe is for a small yield, and it can be doubled.

1 ounce unsweetened chocolate
½ cup sifted unbleached flour
½ teaspoon baking soda
Pinch of salt
1 egg graded "large"
½ teaspoon vanilla extract
⅔ packed cup light brown sugar

Adjust two racks to divide the oven into thirds and preheat oven to 350 degrees. If you have cookie sheets with only one raised rim, those are best for this recipe. Otherwise, use any sheets upside down. Line sheets with baking parchment or aluminum foil, shiny side up.

Place the chocolate in the top of a small double boiler over warm water on moderate heat and let stand until melted. Then remove the top of the double boiler and set aside.

Sift together the flour, baking soda, and salt; set aside.

In a small bowl beat the egg with the vanilla and sugar until thoroughly mixed. Add the chocolate (which may or may not still be warm) and beat to mix. Then add the sifted dry ingredients and beat on low speed to mix.

Transfer the mixture to a small, shallow bowl for ease in handling.

Drop the dough by slightly rounded teaspoonfuls on the lined sheets. Keep the shapes as round and even as you can. Place the cookies about 2 inches apart.

Bake for 10 to 11 minutes, reversing the sheets top to bottom and front to back once during baking to insure even baking. (I have two ovens with clear glass doors. Watching these cookies bake is one of the prettiest sights I know. The cookies behave so well. They rise slightly into perfect shapes. Happiness is baking cookies.)

There is really no way to test these cookies because when they are done they will still feel too soft to the touch. Just watch the clock carefully.

Let the baked cookies stand on the sheets for about a minute, and then slide the paper or foil off the sheets and let the cookies stand until cool.

The cookies will settle down (sink) while cooling.

Remove them with a metal spatula, or just peel the foil or paper away from the backs and place the cookies in an airtight container.

P.S. About the name of this cookie: Luciano Pavarotti recently performed here in Miami Beach. A stage was built on the sand, and thousands of people stood or sat on the beach to hear him. He was superb and the weather was great.

In connection with this event a local hotel created a chocolate dessert in honor of Pavarotti, and they held a contest for someone to name the dessert. They appointed me as judge. They brought me a list of hundreds of names that had been submitted plus several portions of the dessert.

The winning name was Chocolati Pavarotti. It was at the same time that this recipe came about. Chocolati was on my mind.

Chocolate Chip Sour Cream Cookies

24 VERY LARGE COOKIES

This is an all-time comfort food. Big, thick, semisoft, moist, chewy—and loaded with goodies. Whatever you do with these, I suggest that you do not store them in a location that can be seen—or reached. They will disappear too quickly. And frankly, if you don't have strong willpower, maybe you should just not make them.

7½ ounces (1½ cups) raisins
6 ounces (1½ cups) walnuts
2 cups sifted unbleached flour
1 teaspoon baking soda
¼ teaspoon salt
4 ounce (1 stick) unsalted butter
1 teaspoon vanilla extract
1 cup granulated sugar
2 eggs graded "large"
½ cup sour cream
6 ounces (1 cup) semisweet chocolate
    morsels (see Note)

Adjust two racks to divide the oven into thirds and preheat oven to 375 degrees. Line cookie sheets with baking parchment or with aluminum foil, shiny side up.

Steam the raisins as follows: Place them in a vegetable steamer or a strainer over shallow hot water in a saucepan, covered, over high heat. Let the water boil for a few minutes, until the raisins are moist. Remove them from the saucepan and spread out on a piece of foil to air a bit.

Break the nuts into medium-sized pieces; set aside.

Sift together the flour, soda, and salt; set aside.

In the large bowl of an electric mixer beat the butter until soft. Add the vanilla and sugar and beat to mix well. Beat in the eggs and then the sour cream. On low speed gradually add the sifted dry ingredients and beat only until mixed. Remove the bowl from the mixer.

Stir in the raisins, nuts, and chocolate.

Use a heaping tablespoonful of the dough (make these large) for each cookie. Place them at least 2 inches apart (these will spread).

Bake two sheets at a time for 13 to 15 minutes. Reverse the sheets top to bottom and front to back a few times during baking. Watch the cookies on the bottom layer. They might get too dark on the bottom if you don't change the pans top to bottom soon enough. When done, they will be a just barely golden color all over and should just barely spring back when lightly pressed with a fingertip on the top. Do not overbake.

With a wide metal spatula transfer to racks to cool.

If you bake one sheet alone, bake it on the upper of the two racks.

When cool, if you are not going to serve these soon, they should be wrapped as follows: The cookies should be placed two together, bottoms together. Each two cookies may then be wrapped in clear cellophane, wax paper, or aluminum foil, or you can simply put them in a box without wrapping, two together, bottoms together, with wax paper between the layers.

Note: If you wish, you can use cut-up chocolate bars in place of the morsels. I suggest that you use thin 3-ounce bars, for instance, Tobler Tradition or Lindt Excellence, and cut them into pieces a little larger than morsels (someone once said, jokingly, that the chocolate should be cut into chunks any size smaller than the diameter of the cookies). Aim for pieces about ½ inch in diameter, although some will be smaller and some larger.

Sour Cherry and Walnut Chocolate Hermits

32 HUGE COOKIES

Intensely chocolate, with dried pitted sour cherries (raisins can be substituted) and walnuts and a shiny white glaze. Delicious—almost like devil's food cake.

6 ounces (1½ cups) walnuts
2 ounces unsweetened chocolate
1 ounce semisweet chocolate
2½ cups sifted unbleached flour
¾ teaspoon baking soda
2 teaspoons powdered espresso (I use
    Medaglia D'Oro.)
1 tablespoon unsweetened cocoa powder
¼ teaspoon salt
4 ounces (1 stick) unsalted butter
1 teaspoon vanilla extract
1½ packed cups light brown sugar
2 eggs graded "large"
½ cup sour cream
1 tablespoon brandy, prepared coffee, or
    water
4 ounces (1 cup) dried pitted sour cherries

Adjust two racks to divide the oven into thirds and preheat oven to 375 degrees. Line cookie sheets with baking parchment or aluminum foil, shiny side up, and set aside.

Break the walnuts into medium-sized pieces; set aside.

Place both chocolates in the top part of a small double boiler over warm water on moderate heat, and stir occasionally until melted. Remove the top part of the double boiler and set aside.

Sift together the flour, baking soda, espresso, cocoa, and salt; set aside.

In the large bowl of an electric mixer beat the butter until soft. Add the vanilla, then the sugar, and beat until mixed. Beat in the melted chocolate, then the eggs, sour cream, and brandy, coffee, or water. Add the sifted dry ingredients and beat on low speed to mix.

Remove the bowl from the mixer. Stir in the sour cherries and the nuts.

Use a heaping tablespoon of the dough for each cookie. Place the mounds 2 inches apart on the lined cookie sheets.

First, place only one sheet of cookies in the oven on the lower rack. (Set the timer for 13 minutes.) While that first sheet of cookies is baking, prepare the glaze.

GLAZE
¾ cup strained confectioners sugar
1 tablespoon melted butter
1½ tablespoons (or a bit more) heavy or light cream
1 teaspoon vanilla extract
Pinch of salt

In a small bowl beat the above ingredients until smooth. The glaze should be the consistency of mayonnaise; add a bit more cream if necessary. Cover the glaze when you are not using it.

Each sheet of cookies should bake for about 13 minutes.

When the first sheet is half-baked, reverse it front to back and move it to the top rack. At the same time, place another sheet of cookies on the lower rack.

Bake until the cookies spring back when gently pressed with a fingertip. Do not overbake. Watch them, and test them carefully.

As soon as a sheet of cookies is baked, remove it from the oven and place a generous dab (maybe ½ teaspoon) of the glaze on the top of each cookie. As the heat melts the glaze, use a pastry brush to spread it.

Then, with a wide metal spatula, transfer the cookies to a rack to cool.

Continue baking and glazing the cookies.

When the glaze has dried (it dries quickly), the cookies can be stored in an airtight container, two together, bottoms together.

Heath Bar Peanut Butter Cookies

36 TO 40 COOKIES

Today's craze for adding chunks of candy bars and cookies and nuts and whatnot to ice cream (which might have a variety of exotic flavors to begin with) made me wonder what would happen if I added chunks of candy bars and peanuts to peanut butter cookies.

It wasn't as simple as it sounds. When I added peanut brittle, the cookies ran all over the oven. When I added some different candy bars, although the cookies did not run off the sheet and onto the floor of the oven, they did run out on the edges and into each other. Heath bars behaved beautifully.

I suppose you could use large-sized bars since they are going to be cut up anyhow, but I used miniature bars labeled "snack bars." They come in a 9-ounce bag, and I used 1½ bags, which is a generous amount.

14 ounces miniature Heath bars
1½ cups sifted unbleached flour
½ teaspoon baking powder
½ teaspoon baking soda
4 ounces (1 stick) unsalted butter
½ cup smooth or chunky peanut butter
1 teaspoon vanilla
½ packed cup light brown sugar
½ cup granulated sugar
2 eggs graded "large"
4 ounces (1 cup) salted peanuts

Adjust two racks to divide the oven into thirds and preheat oven to 350 degrees. Line cookie sheets with baking parchment or with aluminum foil, shiny side up.

Unwrap the bars of candy and, with a sharp and heavy knife, cut each bar first in half the long way and then crosswise into 3 slices. Set aside.

Sift together the flour, baking powder, and baking soda; set aside.

In the large bowl of an electric mixer beat the butter until soft. Add the peanut butter and vanilla and beat until mixed. Beat in both of the sugars, then the eggs. On low speed add the sifted dry ingredients and beat only until incorporated.

Remove the bowl from the mixer and stir in the candy and the peanuts.

Use a generously rounded tablespoonful of the dough for each cookie. Place the mounds on the lined sheets at least 2 inches apart.

Dip a fork in cold water, and with the cold and wet tines, flatten the tops of the cookies just a bit, making each cookie ½ to ¾ inch thick. Wet the fork again as necessary.

Bake two sheets at a time, reversing the sheets top to bottom and front to back once during baking to insure even baking. Bake about 14 minutes, only until the cookies are lightly colored, not dark. Do not overbake. When done, these will not test done when pressed with a fingertip.

To bake one sheet alone, adjust the rack to the center of the oven and bake about 1 minute less.

With a wide metal spatula transfer to racks to cool.

Store in an airtight container.

Variation

To make Chocolate Chunk Peanut Butter Cookies, use 14 ounces semisweet chocolate in place of the Heath bars. Use thin bars of chocolate (for instance, Tobler Tradition or Lindt Excellence, both of which come in 3-ounce bars). Cut the chocolate into pieces about ½ inch in diameter (make some pieces a little larger). These are heavenly!

Mint Chocolate Cookies

42 COOKIES

This recipe makes 2½ pounds of cookies, a rather large yield.

They are crisp and crunchy, intensely chocolate with a mild and mellow mint flavor. Unusual—and yummy.

4 ounces unsweetened chocolate
8 ounces semisweet chocolate
6 ounces chocolate-covered mints
 (see Note)
1½ cups sifted unbleached flour
½ cup unsweetened cocoa (preferably
 Dutch process)
1 teaspoon baking soda
½ teaspoon salt
6 ounces (1½ sticks) unsalted butter
1 teaspoon vanilla extract
1½ packed cups light brown sugar
3 eggs graded "large"

Adjust two racks to divide the oven into thirds and preheat oven to 325 degrees. Line cookie sheets with baking parchment or with aluminum foil, shiny side up.

Coarsely chop or break up the unsweetened and the semisweet chocolates and the chocolate-covered mints. Place the chocolates and mints in the top part of a large double boiler over warm water on moderate heat. Stir occasionally, until melted. Set aside the top part of the double boiler.

Meanwhile, sift together the flour, cocoa, baking soda, and salt; set aside.

In the large bowl of an electric mixer beat the butter until soft. Add the vanilla and sugar and beat until mixed. Then beat in the eggs, one at a time.

Add the chocolate mixture and beat to mix. (Sometimes little pieces of the mints remain; they don't always melt. The little pieces look great—don't try to remove them.)

On low speed add the sifted dry ingredients and beat to mix. Remove the bowl from the mixer. Stir deeply to be sure everything is mixed.

Use a rounded tablespoon of the dough for each cookie and place the mounds at least 2 inches apart. Do not place more than 5 or 6 on a 12 by 15½-inch cookie sheet.

Bake two sheets at a time for 18 minutes. Reverse the sheets top to bottom and front to back once during baking to insure even baking.

With a wide metal spatula transfer the cookies to racks to cool.

Store in an airtight container.

Note: If you use the York chocolate-covered mint patties, 12 of the small ones equal 6 ounces.

Chef Suki's Almond Lace Cookies

SEE NOTE AS TO YIELD

The only thing better than a great meal is a great meal plus the recipes. My friend Richard Sax invited me to dinner at the deluxe Grand Bay Hotel in Coconut Grove, Florida. Chef Suki prepared a special dinner for us, and it was truly memorable. The last course, a glorious dessert, was a combination of mousse, glacéed chestnuts, several exotic fruits, and this lace wafer (a tuile). These wafers are the thinnest. They are fragile and delicate, like lace, transparent, and about as elegant and classy as a cookie can get. Making these takes time, care, and patience. And they must be stored in an airtight container to remain crisp. But I have kept them successfully for several weeks (in a Rubbermaid freezer box) even here in Miami, where it is always humid.

4 ounces (³/₄ cup) blanched (skinned) almonds
¹/₂ cup granulated sugar
4 ounces (1 stick) unsalted butter
¹/₃ cup light corn syrup
¹/₂ cup plus 2 tablespoons <u>un</u>sifted unbleached flour

Adjust a rack to the center of the oven and preheat oven to 350 degrees. Line cookie sheets with baking parchment or aluminum foil, shiny side up.

Toast the almonds. Place them in a shallow pan in the oven and bake, stirring occasionally, for about 15 minutes, until golden brown. (They taste much better if they are toasted enough.) Let cool.

Place the toasted almonds in the bowl of a food processor fitted with the metal chopping blade. Add the sugar. Pulse the machine 4 or 5 times, then let the motor run for 6 to 8 seconds, until the nuts are chopped into small pieces, but not until they are fine and powdery. They should be about the size of peppercorns or coarse sea salt. Turn the mixture out onto a large piece of paper, spreading it out thinly to see if there are any pieces of nut that are too large. If so, pick them out and cut them into smaller pieces by hand.

In the small bowl of an electric mixer beat the butter until soft. Add the sugar and almond mixture and beat to mix. Beat in the corn syrup, then the flour.

Remove the bowl from the mixer.

The dough will be placed on the lined sheets using a rounded (but not heaping) teaspoonful for each cookie. These will spread wide during baking. Start by placing only 2 on a sheet. Place them far apart. (After you have made a few and you see what they do, you will be able to bake more on one sheet.)

Place a small glass of ice water next to your work space. Dip a teaspoon in the ice water, and use the bottom of the cold and wet spoon to flatten each cookie into a roundish shape from 2 to 3 inches wide. Don't worry about keeping it absolutely round or absolutely level. And don't worry about small holes in the dough.

Bake for 8 to 10 minutes, reversing the sheet front to back once during baking to insure even browning. During baking the dough will bubble up and spread out to a miraculously thin and even layer. WOW! What fun!

If you wish, you can start a second sheet, slightly below the first, when the cookies on the first sheet are half done.

When the cookies are baked to a rich golden brown, remove the sheet from the oven. Do not underbake or they won't be crisp. If all of the cookies are not evenly browned you can remove the sheet from the oven, cool as necessary to remove the cookies that are done, then return the sheet to the oven to continue to bake the others.

Now you have your choice of letting them cool flat on the sheet (then just lifting them off), or you can shape them. They can be shaped in a variety of ways. They can be draped over a rolling pin, they can be wrapped around the handle of a wooden spoon (either side out), or they can be shaped into beautiful cups to serve ice cream and berries in.

If you are making cups, make the cookies slightly larger (or make 2 small cups for each portion, one for ice cream and one for berries, both to be served on the same plate). If you are going to shape them, timing is most important. Pay complete attention to what you are doing. With a wide metal spatula, you will release and transfer them. It can't be done immediately (they will still be too soft and sticky), but if you wait too long they will cool too much and become too brittle to shape. So just stand there and continue trying to move one. As soon as it is ready, you will know. From then on you will have the knack and it will be easy, but slow.

To make a cup shape, turn a custard cup upside down on the work surface. As soon as you can transfer a cookie, place it, either side up, over the bottom of the cup, and with your hands press down on the sides or place another custard cup over the cookie (two custard cups with a cookie in the middle). Once these are shaped, they look charming and turn a scoop of ice cream into a very important celebration.

(Incidentally, Chef Suki left his cookies flat.)

You can wipe the parchment clean with paper towels after using it, and then use it again—and again.

As soon as these have cooled, store them in an airtight container.

Note: I can't tell you what the yield is for this recipe. I have never had the patience to use all of the dough at one time. I made dozens of cookies and then refrigerated or froze the balance of dough for some other time. It lasts very well.

Martha's Vineyard Hermits

36 COOKIES

Recipes for hermits are very old. They probably came with the first settlers. Some are baked in a pan like brownies and then cut into bars. Some are drop cookies like these. Whatever shape they take, they don't get any better than these. Delicious. Loaded with raisins and toasted pecans and flavored with an exotic but mild combination of spices. As soon as these come out of the oven they are brushed with a thin, white glaze that melts and become shiny and dry.

My friends Jan Cowles and Betty and Joe Fleming say these are the best cookies I ever made.

6 ounces (1½ cups) pecans (see Note)
1¾ cups sifted unbleached flour
2 teaspoons ground cinnamon
1 teaspoon ground ginger
½ teaspoon ground nutmeg
¼ teaspoon ground cloves
¼ teaspoon salt
6 ounces (1½ sticks) unsalted butter
1 packed cup light brown sugar
2 eggs graded "large"
3 tablespoons sour cream
¼ teaspoon baking soda
5 ounces (1 cup) raisins

Adjust two racks to divide the oven into thirds and preheat oven to 350 degrees. Line cookie sheets with baking parchment or aluminum foil, shiny side up, and set aside.

First, toast the pecans in a shallow pan in the oven for 10 to 13 minutes, stirring once or twice, until they are very hot to the touch but not darker in color. Cool and then break into large pieces; set aside.

Sift together the flour, cinnamon, ginger, nutmeg, cloves, and salt; set aside.

In the large bowl of an electric mixer beat the butter until soft. Add the sugar and beat until well mixed. Beat in the eggs, one at a time. In a small cup, stir the sour cream and baking soda to mix well, then beat it into the butter mixture. Add the sifted dry ingredients and beat on low speed only until incorporated. Remove the bowl from the mixer.

Stir in the raisins and nuts.

Use a rounded tablespoon of the dough for each cookie. Place the mounds at least 2 inches apart on the lined cookie sheets.

First, place only one sheet of cookies in the oven on the lower rack. While that first sheet of cookies is baking, prepare the glaze.

GLAZE
¾ cup sifted confectioners sugar
1 tablespoon soft butter (salted or unsalted)
1½ tablespoons or a bit more light or heavy cream
1 teaspoon vanilla extract
Pinch of salt

In a small bowl beat the above ingredients until smooth; the glaze should be the consistency of mayonnaise. Add a bit more cream if necessary. Cover the glaze when you are not using it.

Each sheet of cookies should bake for 10 to 15 minutes, until lightly browned and until they spring back when gently pressed with a fingertip.

When the first sheet is half baked, move it to the top rack, and reverse it front to back. At the same time, place another sheet of cookies on the lower rack.

As soon as a sheet of cookies is baked, remove it from the oven and place a generous dab (maybe ½ teaspoon) of the glaze on top of each cookie. As the heat melts the glaze, use a pastry brush to spread it over the cookie.

Then, with a wide metal spatula transfer the cookies to a rack to cool. When the glaze has dried (it takes only a few minutes) the cookies can be stored in an airtight container.

Continue baking, and glazing, the cookies as above.

Note: If you wish, walnuts can be used instead of pecans. Walnuts do not have to be toasted but they may be; toasting makes them more crisp.

Walnut Jumbles

ABOUT 27 COOKIES

Soft, tender, delicate, irresistibly delicious old-fashioned cookies. And they are quick and easy.

Jumbles are very old; there are recipes for them in the earliest cookbooks, and this is the best recipe I know of for them.

5 ounces (1¼ cups) walnuts
1⅔ cups sifted unbleached flour
¼ teaspoon baking soda
1 teaspoon baking powder
Scant ½ teaspoon salt
3 ounces (¾ stick) unsalted butter
⅔ cup granulated sugar
1 egg graded "large"
½ cup sour cream

Adjust two racks to divide the oven into thirds and preheat oven to 400 degrees. Line cookie sheets with baking parchment or aluminum foil, shiny side up.

Break the walnuts into large pieces; set aside.

Sift together the flour, baking soda, baking powder, and salt; set aside.

In the small bowl of an electric mixer beat the butter until soft. Add the sugar and beat to mix. Beat in the egg. On low speed beat in half the sifted dry ingredients. Then beat in the sour cream, then the remaining sifted dry ingredients. Remove the bowl from the mixer.

Stir in the nuts.

Use a heaping teaspoonful of the dough for each cookie, and place them 2 inches apart on the lined cookie sheets.

TOPPING
1 tablespoon granulated sugar
½ teaspoon ground cinnamon

In a small cup mix the sugar and cinnamon and sprinkle generously over the cookies.

Bake two sheets at a time for about 12 minutes, reversing them once top to bottom and front to back to insure even baking. When done, the cookies will be a pale golden color and will spring back when gently pressed on top with a fingertip.

With a wide metal spatula transfer the cookies to racks to cool.

If you are baking only one sheet at a time, adjust the rack to the center of the oven, and place the cookie sheet on top of another cookie sheet to prevent the bottoms from becoming too dark.

Because these are soft, store them two together, bottoms together, or they might lose their shape.

Store in an airtight container.

Jumbo Raisin and Sour Cherry Cookies

14 REALLY LARGE COOKIES

Extra-large, thick, and semisoft, totally delicious, plain old-fashioned cookies loaded with a heap of raisins and sour cherries (or, if you wish, use 2 cups of raisins and no cherries).

2½ cups plus 2 tablespoons sifted unbleached flour
¼ teaspoon baking soda
¼ teaspoon salt
4 ounces (1 stick) unsalted butter
1 cup granulated sugar
1 egg plus 1 additional egg white graded "large"
½ cup heavy cream
5 ounces (1 cup) raisins
5 ounces (1 cup) dried pitted sour cherries

Adjust an oven rack to the top position (it is best to bake these only one sheet at a time) and preheat oven to 400 degrees. These should be baked on double cookie sheets—place one on top of another and line the top one with baking parchment. Set aside.

Sift together the flour, baking soda, and salt; set aside. In the large bowl of an electric mixer beat the butter until soft. Add the sugar and the egg and egg white and beat to mix. On low speed add about half the sifted dry ingredients and beat to mix. Add the heavy cream and beat to mix, then add the remaining dry ingredients and beat only until incorporated. Finally, beat in the raisins and cherries.

Remove the bowl from the mixer and stir the ingredients a bit with a large rubber or wooden spatula to be sure the raisins and cherries are thoroughly distributed.

Have a wide glass or a small bowl of ice water next to you.

To divide the dough into cookies it is best to use an ice cream scoop that is 2 inches in diameter and has a ¼-cup capacity. Dip the scoop in the ice water before scooping up each cookie. Shake off the water.

Fill the scoop level, not mounded high. Otherwise, use a heaping tablespoonful for each cookie, and try to keep the shapes as even as you can.

Place the cookies 3 inches apart on the lined sheets.

Then dip a fork in the ice water and press several times in all directions on the top of each cookie to flatten it to about a ½-inch thickness and a scant 3 inches in diameter. Dip the fork in the ice water frequently.

Bake one sheet at a time on the upper rack for about 16 or 17 minutes, reversing the sheet front to back once or twice during baking. When done, the cookies should be golden brown (these are best if they are not too pale) and should spring back when gently pressed with a fingertip.

With a wide metal spatula transfer the cookies to racks to cool.

Store the cookies two together, bottoms together. Store in an airtight container.

All-Bran Raisin Oatmeal Cookies

ABOUT 24 4- TO 4½-INCH COOKIES

Monsters! Crisp and chewy, loaded with raisins and some peanut butter.

1 cup sifted all-purpose whole wheat flour (Any flour that is too coarse to go through the sifter should be stirred back into the sifted part.)

1 teaspoon baking soda

¼ teaspoon salt

8 ounces (2 sticks) unsalted butter

½ cup smooth or chunky peanut butter

1¼ packed cups light brown sugar

¾ cup All-Bran cereal

2 eggs graded "large"

1 teaspoon vanilla extract

13 ounces (2½ cups) raisins

2 cups old-fashioned (not "instant") oatmeal

Adjust two racks to divide the oven into thirds and preheat oven to 350 degrees. Line cookie sheets with baking parchment or with aluminum foil, shiny side up, and set aside.

Sift together the flour, baking soda, and salt (any flour that is too coarse to go through the sifter should be stirred back into the sifted ingredients); set aside.

In a heavy saucepan with about a 4- to 6-cup capacity, melt the butter over medium heat. Add the peanut butter and sugar and stir for a few minutes over the heat to partially melt the sugar. Remove from the heat. Stir in the All-Bran. Transfer to a large mixing bowl and let stand.

In a small bowl beat the eggs and vanilla just to mix. Add to the butter mixture and stir to mix thoroughly. Stir in the raisins. Stir in the oatmeal and the sifted dry ingredients.

Each cookie should be made of ¼ cup dough. You can use either a large spoon, a ¼-cup measuring cup, or—and this is best—an ice cream scoop. The scoop that measures 2 inches in diameter is a good size for these. Place the cookies at least 2½ inches apart (these spread) on the lined sheets, no more than 6 cookies on a 12 by 15½-inch sheet.

Place a cup of cold water next to your work space. Dip a table fork in the water, and with the underside of the wet fork flatten each cookie to a ½-inch thickness by pressing first in one direction and then in the opposite direction. Wet the fork as often as necessary.

Bake two sheets at a time for about 15 minutes, reversing the sheets top to bottom and front to back once during baking. After about 15 minutes the cookies will be lightly colored all over. Remove the sheets from the oven and let the cookies stand for a few minutes, until firm enough to be moved. With a wide metal spatula transfer the cookies to racks to cool.

If you bake one sheet alone, adjust an oven rack to the center of the oven, and reverse the sheet front to back once during baking.

When cool, store the cookies in an airtight container. It is best to store them two together, bottoms together.

Light-As-Air* Cookies

These are most unusual. They are extremely simple, plain, and light, wonderful with tea or alongside a fruit, custard, or ice cream dessert. Children adore them—everyone does.

30 COOKIES

2 eggs graded "large"
1 teaspoon vanilla extract
1 cup granulated sugar
1½ teaspoons baking powder
1¾ cups sifted unbleached flour

Adjust an oven rack to the middle of the oven and preheat oven to 375 degrees. Line cookie sheets with baking parchment or with aluminum foil, shiny side up; set aside.

In the small bowl of an electric mixer beat the eggs, vanilla, and sugar at high speed for a few minutes until the mixture is pale and thick enough to form a ribbon when the beaters are raised. Then, on low speed, add the baking powder and the flour and beat only until incorporated.

Transfer the mixture to a smaller bowl for ease in handling.

Use a rounded tablespoonful of the batter for each cookie. Keep the shapes neat and round, not ragged. Place the cookies 1½ to 2 inches apart.

All the batter should be shaped immediately, even though some of the sheets will stand and wait since these are baked only 1 sheet at a time. (If you let the batter remain in the bowl for a while it will thicken too much to be formed into neat shapes.) If you don't have enough cookie sheets (probably 3), shape the cookies anyway, on parchment or foil placed on any work surface. Then, right before baking, slide a cookie sheet under the parchment or foil.

Bake one sheet at a time for 11 minutes, reversing the sheet front to back once during baking to ensure even baking. When done, the cookies will be dry and firm on the tops but will be as soft as soft mac-

* not really

aroons inside. When done, the cookies will be a pale, pale sandy color.

With a wide metal spatula transfer the cookies to racks to cool.

Store in an airtight container. If you serve them within a day or two, they will have a divine, moist texture inside. After a few days they become more crisp. They are popular both ways, but I like them very fresh.

Note: If you let these stand on the cookie sheet for 2 to 3 hours before baking, something strange takes place—a firm crust forms on the tops of the cookies. Then, during baking, as the cookies rise a little, this firm crust slides off slightly to one side. It doesn't affect the taste, but the cookies become very exotic looking. They look as though they were made of two different doughs. It's fascinating. I think no one will be able to guess how you did it.

Cookies that have waited for 2 or 3 hours before baking should be baked for only 9 or 10 minutes.

Saturday Night Meringues

This is a quickie. They bake for only 10 minutes, and it doesn't take much more time than that to mix and shape them. Like all meringues, these have no butter, oil, or egg yolks, but these are intensely chocolate with moist and chewy centers.

32 COOKIES

6 ounces semisweet chocolate
3½ ounces (1 cup) walnuts
2 egg whites from eggs graded "large"
Pinch of salt
½ cup granulated sugar
½ teaspoon vanilla extract
1 teaspoon lemon juice or ½ teaspoon cider vinegar

Adjust two racks to divide the oven into thirds and preheat oven to 350 degrees. Line two large cookie sheets with baking parchment or with aluminum foil, shiny side up.

Break or cut up the chocolate and place it in the top part of a small double boiler over shallow hot water on moderate heat. Cover with a paper towel (to absorb steam) and the pot cover. Stir occasionally until melted. Remove the top part of the double boiler and set aside, uncovered, to cool a bit.

Break the nuts into medium-sized pieces; set aside.

In the small bowl of an electric mixer beat the whites with the salt until they barely hold a soft mound (not a point) when the beaters are raised. On medium speed, gradually add the sugar, one rounded teaspoonful at a time, beating for a few seconds between additions.

When about half the sugar has been added, add the vanilla and lemon juice or vinegar, and continue to add the sugar.

When all the sugar has been added, increase the speed to high and beat on low until the whites hold a firm point when the beaters are raised.

Remove the bowl from the mixer. Add the chocolate all at once. With a rubber spatula fold together the whites and the chocolate. Do not handle any more than necessary. It is not necessary to fold until you don't see any more whites; actually, it looks nice to see a few streaks of white.

Gently fold in the nuts.

Use a rounded teaspoonful of the meringue for each cookie, using one teaspoon for picking up and one for pushing off. Place the mounds on the lined sheets about 1½ inches apart.

Bake for 10 minutes. (While baking these meringues I do not reverse the sheets; these don't seem to need it.)

When done, if you have baked on parchment, you will be able to lift the cookies with your fingers. Just turn them on their sides or upside down to cool. If you have baked on foil, you might need a spatula to help remove them and turn them over.

Cool and then store in an airtight container.

Hungarian Walnut Kisses

This crisp and tender meringue is cooked before it is shaped, then it is shaped with two spoons, like drop cookies, and baked for about 2½ hours.

I love meringues, and I've made every recipe I know of. This one is less fragile (although it is tender) and less difficult—and safer—than others I've made. Home-made meringues are very special.

ABOUT 24 VERY LARGE
MERINGUE COOKIES

5 ounces (1½ cups) walnuts
4 egg whites from eggs graded "large" (To measure ½ cup; they
    may be whites that were frozen and then thawed.)
⅛ teaspoon salt
¼ teaspoon cream of tartar
1 tablespoon lemon juice
½ teaspoon vanilla extract
1½ cups granulated sugar

Adjust two racks to divide the oven into thirds and preheat oven to 250 degrees. Cut aluminum foil to fit two cookie sheets; set aside.

Cut the nuts into medium or small pieces; set aside.

Place all the ingredients except the nuts in the top part of a large double boiler (it should have about an 8-cup capacity). Place over hot water on moderate heat and beat with a portable electric mixer for about 7 minutes.

Transfer the mixture to the large bowl of an electric mixer and beat at high speed for 5 to 7 minutes, scraping the sides frequently with a rubber spatula, until the mixture is firm enough to hold a straight point when the beaters are raised. It will be a thick marshmallow mixture, as smooth and shiny as satin. (Actually, it is a gorgeous 7-minute icing.)

To hold the aluminum foil in place, spread a bit of the meringue near each corner of the cookie sheets. Cover the sheets with the foil, shiny side up, and press firmly on the corners.

Fold the nuts into the meringue.

Use a heaping (mounded high) tablespoon of the meringue for each cookie. Use one spoon for picking up and another for pushing off. Place about 12 mounds on each sheet.

Bake for 1½ hours, reversing the sheets top to bottom and front to back once during baking to insure even baking. Then turn off the heat, but do not remove the meringues from the oven. They should remain in the turned-off oven for up to an hour, but you must keep an eye on them. They should not color any more than a pale, pale golden color, and even though the heat is off they will continue to bake. When they color slightly, or when the hour is up, remove them from the oven and lift them carefully from the foil. Some of these might crack slightly during baking—this is to be expected.

Store carefully in an airtight box. A Rubbermaid freezer box is safe for these.

Sweet and Hot Meringues

20 TO 22 MERINGUES

Meringues are pretty la-de-da to begin with, but these—loaded with macadamia nuts and candied ginger—are especially elegant, regal, extravagant, extraordinary, and delicious.

It is best to make meringues when the climate is dry and not humid. But I make these often in Miami Beach where I live and where it is almost always humid, and they are always perfectly dry and crisp and crunchy.

Making these is easy and fun, but baking them and drying them is slow and takes a long time.

7½ ounces (1½ cups) roasted and salted macadamia nuts (I use the Mauna Loa nuts in a jar—they are roasted and salted.)
2½ ounces candied ginger (to make a generous ⅓ cup when cut into small pieces)
½ cup plus ½ teaspoon granulated sugar
2 egg whites from eggs graded "large"
Scant ⅛ teaspoon salt
½ teaspoon vanilla extract
⅛ teaspoon cream of tartar (see Note)

Adjust two racks to divide the oven into thirds and preheat the oven to 225 degrees. (Check the temperature with a portable oven thermometer—it is important not to bake these in a hotter oven.) Line two cookie sheets with baking parchment or aluminum foil, shiny side up. Set aside.

Place the nuts in a wide strainer and shake it over the sink to remove excess salt. Cut the macadamia nuts (I do it one at a time), cutting each nut into approximate halves. Place the nuts in a medium-size mixing bowl and set aside.

Cut the ginger (I do it with scissors) into uneven pieces from ¼ to ½ inch in diameter and place in a small bowl. Add ½ teaspoon of the sugar (reserve remaining ½ cup sugar) and stir to coat the pieces of ginger so they do not stick together.

Add the ginger to the nuts and toss or stir to mix.

Place the egg whites, salt, vanilla, and cream of tartar in the small bowl of an electric mixer. Beat on moderate speed for about half a minute until the whites hold a soft point (one that bends over) when the beaters are raised. Then reduce the speed to low and start to add the sugar. Add 1 rounded tablespoonful at a time, beating for a few seconds between additions. When all the sugar has been added, increase the speed to high and beat for 1½ to 2 minutes until the meringue holds a very firm shape but is still shiny.

Add the meringue to the nuts and ginger. Fold together gently and carefully—do not handle any more than necessary—only until the nuts and ginger are incorporated.

Use a well-rounded tablespoon of the meringue for each cookie. Use 1 spoon for picking up the meringue and another for pushing it off. High peaks of the meringue are beautiful. Place the meringues at least an inch apart on the lined sheets. Work quickly and do not handle any more than necessary.

Bake for 1½ hours, reversing the sheets top to bottom and front to back once during baking to insure even baking. The meringues should not color any more than a pale eggshell off-white. Look at them frequently and, if necessary, reduce the oven temperature a bit. After 1½ hours the meringues should be dry enough for you to be able to lift one from the parchment or foil without having it stick. But if not, continue to bake a bit longer. Total baking time should be 1½ to 2 hours.

Then turn the heat off and let the meringues stand in the oven with the door closed for 1 hour. After that, prop the oven door open about 2 or 3 inches (I hold it open with a rolled up pot holder) and let stand until the meringues are cool (this might take another hour or so).

Lift the cooled meringues with your fingers and place them in an airtight container (I use Rubbermaid boxes). Cover each layer of the meringues loosely with plastic wrap and close the box securely.

Note: To measure ⅛ teaspoon cream of tartar, first measure a level ¼ teaspoon. Then cut half of it away and return it to the container. Use the ⅛ teaspoon remaining in the measuring spoon.

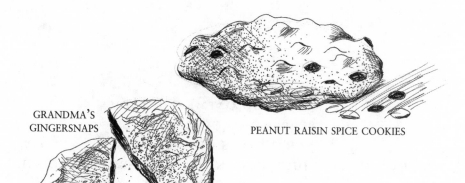

GRANDMA'S
GINGERSNAPS

PEANUT RAISIN SPICE COOKIES

Cookies That Are Dropped and Rolled Between Your Hands

CHOCOLATE CHUNK COCONUT
PEANUT BUTTER COOKIES

THE $250.00 COOKIE RECIPE

KEY LARGO OATMEAL COOKIES
PEPPER AND GINGER WAFERS
GRANDMA'S GINGERSNAPS
CHOCOLATE-CHUNK-COCONUT-PEANUT-BUTTER COOKIES
CHOCOLATE FONDANT COOKIES
CHOCOLATE LULUS
SOUTHERN CHOCOLATE PEANUT COOKIES
BLACK WALNUT PEARLS
PEANUT RAISIN SPICE COOKIES
THE $250.00 COOKIE RECIPE
POSITIVELY-THE-ABSOLUTELY-BEST-
CHOCOLATE-CHIP COOKIES

Key Largo Oatmeal Cookies

36 LARGE COOKIES

These ingredients include potato chips. The recipe is from a small bakery in the Florida Keys (the bakery is close to the spot where Humphrey Bogart and Lauren Bacall made the famous movie, *Key Largo,* in 1948). I have no idea how the potato chips came about, but hey, why not? (Maybe the bakery was out of chocolate chips and substituted potato chips. Chips are chips. Or maybe they were out of salt.)

These are large and substantial, crisp and crunchy, with raisins, sour cherries (which are optional), and nuts, and if you don't tell anyone about the potato chips, they will never guess.

4 ounces salted potato chips
6 ounces (1½ cups) walnuts
2 cups sifted unbleached flour
1 teaspoon baking soda
8 ounces (2 sticks) unsalted butter
1 teaspoon vanilla extract
1¾ packed cups light brown sugar
2 eggs graded "large"
2 cups old-fashioned (not "instant") oatmeal
5 ounces (1 cup) raisins
5 ounces (1 cup) dried pitted sour cherries (see Note)

Adjust two racks to divide the oven into thirds and preheat oven to 350 degrees. Line cookie sheets with baking parchment or aluminum foil, shiny side up, and set aside.

Place the potato chips in a plastic or paper bag and squeeze the bag a few times with both hands to break the pieces just a bit; they should be coarse, not fine. They should measure 2 packed cups. Set aside.

Break the walnuts into large pieces; set aside.

Sift together the flour and baking soda; set aside.

In the large bowl of an electric mixer beat the butter until soft. Add the vanilla and sugar and beat until mixed. Add the eggs and beat to mix. Then add the sifted dry ingredients and beat on low speed only until incorporated. Add the oatmeal and beat to mix. Remove the bowl from the mixer.

Transfer the dough to a larger bowl (if you don't have one, you can do this in the same bowl—just not as easily). With a heavy, wooden spatula stir in the raisins, cherries, and nuts. Finally stir in the potato chips. The chips should still be visible. This takes a strong arm and some heavy stirring.

Each cookie should be made of ¼ cup dough. You can use two spoons and guess at the amount, a ¼-cup measuring cup, or (this is best) a small ice cream scoop (the scoop that measures 2 inches in diameter is the right size).

Place a large piece of aluminum foil next to the sink, and place the mounds any which way on the foil. Then wet your hands under cold water, shake them off but do not dry them, and with your damp hands roll a mound of dough into a ball, flatten it to about a ¾-inch thickness, and place it on a lined sheet. Continue to shape the cookies, and place them 2 inches apart (no more than 6 on a 12 by 15½-inch sheet). Keep your hands damp as necessary.

Bake two sheets at a time for 18 to 20 minutes, reversing the sheets top to bottom and front to back twice during baking. (If you leave one sheet on the lower rack for too long, those cookies might become too dark on the bottoms.) When done, the cookies should be lightly browned all over. Do not overbake.

If you bake one sheet alone, bake it on the higher of the two racks, and reverse it front to back once or twice during baking. When you bake one sheet alone, the cookies will bake in less time.

Let them cool briefly, then with a wide metal spatula transfer them to racks to cool.

These can be stored in an airtight box or they can be wrapped two together (bottoms together) in clear cellophane, wax paper, or aluminum foil. (Always store these two together, bottoms together.)

· · ·

Note: You can substitute raisins for the cherries, or dried cranberries, or cut-up dates, or cut-up dried apricots, or a combination. But the sour cherries are the best. They can be bought at many specialty food stores, or they can be ordered from American Spoon Foods in Petoskey, Michigan (800-222-5886).

Pepper and Ginger Wafers

30 TO 32 3½-INCH
COOKIES

Very thin, both crisp and chewy. They are delicious (addictive), and with something to drink or vanilla ice cream, there's no stopping. I'm helpless.

2½ cups sifted unbleached flour
2 teaspoons baking soda
3 teaspoons ground ginger
¼ teaspoon salt
½ teaspoon finely ground black or white pepper (preferably freshly ground)
6 ounces (1½ sticks) unsalted butter
1 cup granulated sugar
1 egg graded "large"
1 teaspoon vinegar
¼ cup light honey

Adjust two racks to divide the oven into thirds and preheat oven to 350 degrees. Line cookie sheets with baking parchment (preferably) or aluminum foil, shiny side up (OK if necessary).

Sift together the flour, baking soda, ginger, salt, and pepper; set aside.

In the large bowl of an electric mixer beat the butter until soft, then add the sugar and beat to mix.

Beat in the egg, vinegar, and honey. Then, on low speed, gradually add the dry ingredients; beat until mixed, scraping the bowl frequently with a rubber spatula. Transfer to a small bowl for ease in handling.

Place a length of aluminum foil next to the sink. Use a rounded tablespoon of the dough for each cookie. Place them any which way on the foil. Wet your hands with cold water. Shake them off a bit but do not dry them. Roll the mounds of dough between your wet hands into ball shapes about 1½ inches in diameter. Wet your hands again frequently.

Place the balls 3 inches apart (these spread) on the lined sheets (I place 8 cookies on a 17 by 14-inch sheet).

Bake two sheets at time for 12 to 14 minutes, reversing the sheets top to bottom and front to back once during baking to insure even browning. When done, the cookies should be colored all over. If they are still pale in the centers, bake a bit longer or just let the cookies stand a bit on the hot sheets. Do not underbake.

When done, if a few are still not quite done in the centers, they can be put back in the oven for a minute or two.

During baking these will rise a bit and then flatten when done.

Let cool briefly on the sheets and then, with a metal spatula, transfer to racks to cool.

When cool, store in an airtight container.

Grandma's Gingersnaps

22 COOKIES

My friend Maryam Mohit and I were waiting for our car at a hotel in Coral Gables, Florida, when a lady we didn't know asked us for a lift. During our long wait, I happened to mention that I was writing a cookie book. She said she had a great cookie recipe that had been in her family a long time, and if we would give her a lift, she would give me the recipe. Her name is Jennifer Moyer and I am indeed grateful to her for this terrific cookie. I'll swap a ride any day—or every day—for a recipe this good.

The cookies are thin, unusually moist and chewy, and spiced to perfection.

2½ cups sifted unbleached flour
½ teaspoon salt
2 teaspoons baking soda
1 teaspoon ground ginger
1 teaspoon ground cinnamon
½ teaspoon ground cloves
3 ounces (¾ stick) unsalted butter
1 packed cup light brown sugar
1 egg graded "large"
¼ cup light and mild molasses
Granulated sugar (to roll the cookies in)

Adjust a rack to the middle of the oven and preheat oven to 375 degrees. Line cookie sheets with baking parchment or with aluminum foil, shiny side up, and set aside.

Sift together the flour, salt, baking soda, ginger, cinnamon, and cloves; set aside.

In the large bowl of an electric mixer beat the butter and brown sugar until smooth. Add the egg and molasses and beat until perfectly smooth. Gradually add the sifted dry ingredients and beat on low speed only until incorporated. Transfer the mixture to a small bowl for ease in handling.

Place 1 to 2 cups of granulated sugar on a dinner plate.

Spread out a length of aluminum foil or wax paper.

Form the dough into 22 mounds using a rounded teaspoonful of dough for each cookie; place them any which way on the foil or wax paper.

(The dough will be very soft. It must be handled gently!) Pick up a mound and roll it between your hands into a ball; place it on the sugar. Repeat a few times, placing a few mounds on the sugar. Roll them, one at a time, to coat all over, and place them 3 inches apart on a lined sheet. Sprinkle additional sugar generously on top of each mound. (Remaining sugar may be strained and returned to your sugar container.)

Bake one sheet at a time for 8½ minutes, reversing the sheet front to back once during baking. The cookies will not look done—but they are best if they are soft and not crisp. Do not overbake.

Let the cookies cool on the sheet for a minute or so, then transfer them with a wide spatula to a rack to cool.

Repeat until all the cookies are baked.

Store the cookies in an airtight container. These must be stored flat or they will lose their shape.

Chocolate-Chunk-Coconut-Peanut-Butter Cookies

32 COOKIES

Especially crisp, crunchy, and chewy. They taste like chocolate chip macaroons. Everybody loves them.

6 ounces semisweet chocolate (I use two 3-ounce bars of Ghirardelli dark chocolate; see Note.)
4 ounces (1 cup) salted peanuts
½ cup granulated sugar
1¼ cups sifted unbleached flour
½ teaspoon baking powder
½ teaspoon baking soda
4 ounces (1 stick) unsalted butter
1 teaspoon vanilla extract
½ cup smooth or chunky peanut butter
1 tablespoon sour cream
½ packed cup dark or light brown sugar
1 egg graded "large"
3½ ounces (1 packed cup) shredded coconut

Adjust two racks to divide the oven into thirds and preheat oven to 375 degrees. Line cookie sheets with baking parchment or aluminum foil, shiny side up, and set aside.

On a board, with a long and sharp knife, cut the chocolate into pieces about ½ inch in diameter; set aside.

Place the peanuts and granulated sugar in the bowl of a food processor fitted with the metal chopping blade. Pulse the machine five times, until the nuts are chopped into large pieces. Set aside.

Sift together the flour, baking powder, and baking soda; set aside.

In the large bowl of an electric mixer beat the butter until soft. Beat in the vanilla, peanut butter, and sour cream. Beat in the brown sugar and the egg. Add the sifted dry ingredients and beat on low speed until mixed.

Remove the bowl from the mixer and stir in the peanut mixture, the cut-up chocolate, and the coconut.

Place a large piece of aluminum foil next to the sink. With two spoons, form the dough into mounds, using a slightly rounded table-spoonful for each cookie and placing them any which way on the foil.

Then wet your hands with cold water. Shake them off but do not dry them. One at a time, roll the mounds into balls; place them about 2 inches apart on the lined sheets. Continue to wet your hands as necessary.

Dip a fork into cold water and, with the back of the tines, press gently on each cookie to flatten it to about a ½-inch thickness. Press the cookies in only one direction. Wet the fork often.

Bake two sheets at a time for 12 to 15 minutes, reversing the sheets top to bottom and front to back once during baking. When done, the cookies should be lightly browned, but the tops will not test done if you press them with a fingertip; they will still feel quite soft. They will become crisp when cool.

With a wide metal spatula transfer cookies to racks to cool.

Store in an airtight container.

Note: I really have nothing against chocolate morsels—I have probably used bushels of them, and I adore Toll House Chocolate Chip Cookies. But once you get in the habit of using a delicious chocolate bar, cut into pieces much larger than morsels, you will love it. It will make a whole different cookie. You can cut up chocolate bars for any recipe that calls for morsels, and vice versa.

Chocolate Fondant Cookies

Beautifully plain, round cookies. Simple—but classy and unusual. Semisoft and intensely chocolate. They have both milk chocolate and cocoa.

3 1/2 ounces (7 tablespoons) unsalted butter
3/4 cup sifted unbleached flour
1 teaspoon baking powder
Pinch of salt
1/3 cup unsweetened cocoa powder (I use Dutch process.)
1/3 cup granulated sugar
7 ounces milk chocolate (I have made these with a plain Hershey bar and also with Hershey Symphony—both are delicious.)
2 eggs graded "large"
Optional: Confectioners sugar (to sprinkle on just before serving)

Adjust a rack one-fourth or one-third down from the top of the oven (the bottoms of the cookies might become too dark if you bake them any lower—that's also why I bake these only one sheet at a time). Preheat the oven to 350 degrees. Line cookie sheets with aluminum foil, shiny side up, or with baking parchment.

Cut the butter into small pieces; set aside.

Place the flour, baking powder, salt, cocoa, and sugar in the bowl of a food processor fitted with the chopping blade. Pulse the machine briefly to mix. Cut or break the chocolate into small pieces and add. Process for 20 seconds, until the chocolate is in tiny pieces.

Add the butter and process for 15 to 20 seconds, until the ingredients begin to hold together.

With the motor running add the eggs through the feed tube and process for about 5 seconds, until well mixed. If the mixture is lumpy, stir it a bit to break up the lumps and then process again until mixed. Transfer the mixture to a small bowl.

Place a piece of foil next to the sink. Place the dough by rounded tablespoonfuls any which way on the foil. Wet your hands with cold water. Shake them off but do not dry them. With wet hands pick up a mound of dough and roll it between your hands into a ball. Place on a lined cookie sheet. Continue to shape the balls and place them on the sheet 2⅓ to 3 inches apart.

Bake for about 14 or 15 minutes, reversing the sheet front to back once during baking to insure even baking. To test for doneness press the top of a cookie gently with your fingertip; when the dough just barely springs back, the cookies are done. Watch carefully—do not overbake.

With a wide metal spatula transfer the cookies to a rack to cool.

Store two together, bottoms together, in an airtight container.

Optional: just before serving, sprinkle lightly with confectioners sugar through a fine strainer.

Chocolate Lulus

These are delicious and fun to make. They are very dark chocolate, crisp and crunchy, with just a bit of pepper, which no one recognizes. But people ask, "What is this wonderful chocolate?" The pepper does that.

36 COOKIES

3 ounces semisweet chocolate
4 ounces (1 stick) unsalted butter
½ firmly packed cup light brown sugar
1½ cups sifted unbleached flour
½ teaspoon baking soda
2 tablespoons unsweetened cocoa powder
Pinch of salt
¼ teaspoon finely ground black or white
   pepper (preferably freshly ground)
1 egg graded "large"
1 teaspoon vanilla extract
Granulated sugar (for coating the cookies)

Adjust an oven rack to the center of the oven and preheat oven to 350 degrees. Line cookie sheets with baking parchment or aluminum foil, shiny side up.

Chop or break the chocolate into pieces. Place the chocolate and the butter in a medium-sized heavy saucepan over moderate heat. Stir frequently until melted. Add the brown sugar and continue to stir for a minute or two over the heat. Remove from the heat and let stand.

Sift together the flour, baking soda, cocoa, salt, and pepper; set aside.

In a large bowl beat the egg and vanilla just to mix. Add the chocolate mixture (which may or may not still be warm); and stir to mix. Add the sifted dry ingredients and stir to mix. Transfer to a shallow bowl for ease in handling.

Place a large piece of aluminum foil on the work surface. Drop rounded teaspoons of the dough any which way, close to each other on the foil.

Place some granulated sugar in a wide and shallow bowl (a wide soup dish or a spaghetti dish). Pick up a mound of the dough and roll it between your hands into a smooth, round ball 1 inch in diameter. Place it on the granulated sugar. Continue shaping about 6 balls. Roll them around in the sugar to coat. Place them on the lined sheet, 2 inches apart. Continue, placing 12 on the sheet.

Now, with a table fork, press on each cookie in one direction, only to flatten it. The flattened cookies should be 1½ inches wide and ½ inch thick.

When you have finished shaping all the cookies, the remaining sugar may be strained and returned to the sugar jar.

Bake one sheet at a time for about 12 minutes, reversing the sheet front to back once during baking to insure even baking. These are so dark it will be difficult to see if they are browning. Do not overbake. After 12 minutes of baking they should just feel semi-firm on the edges, and they might still feel slightly soft in the centers. They will crisp as they cool.

Continue to shape and bake the remaining cookies.

Store in an airtight container.

Southern Chocolate Peanut Cookies

30 TO 35 COOKIES

Crisp and crunchy, dark chocolate peanut butter cookies loaded with chunks of milk chocolate and a ton of peanuts, you all.

6 ounces milk chocolate
¾ cup sifted unbleached flour
⅓ cup unsweetened cocoa power (preferably Dutch process)
1 teaspoon baking soda
4 ounces (1 stick) unsalted butter
½ cup smooth or chunky peanut butter
½ teaspoon vanilla extract
1 firmly packed cup light brown sugar
1 egg graded "large"
8 ounces (generous 1½ cups) salted peanuts (I use honey-roasted or dry-roasted.)

Adjust two racks to divide the oven into thirds and preheat oven to 350 degrees. Line cookie sheets with baking parchment; set aside.

Place the chocolate on a cutting board, and with a long and sharp knife cut the chocolate into pieces about ¼ inch (or a little larger) in diameter. Set aside.

Sift together the flour, cocoa, and baking soda; set aside.

In the large bowl of an electric mixer beat the butter until soft. Add the peanut butter and vanilla and beat to mix. Beat in the sugar, then the egg, and finally, on low speed, the sifted dry ingredients.

Remove the bowl from the mixer. Add the cut-up chocolate and the peanuts, and stir—and stir—and stir until mixed.

Place a large piece of aluminum foil next to the sink. Use a heaping teaspoonful of the dough for each cookie. Place mounds of the dough any which way on the foil.

Wet your hands with cold water; shake them off but do not dry them. With wet hands pick up a mound of the dough, roll it between your hands to make a ball, flatten it slightly, and place it on a lined cookie sheet. Continue to shape the cookies, and place them about 2 inches apart. Wet your hands occasionally as necessary.

Bake two sheets at a time, reversing the sheets top to bottom and front to back once during baking. Bake for 12 minutes. These will still feel too soft, but don't bother to test them—they will become firm when cool. They will rise a bit during baking and then will flatten when cool.

It is best to bake these two sheets at a time, but if you must bake one sheet alone, bake it on the upper of the two racks.

Let the baked cookies stand on the sheets for a scant minute, then transfer them with a wide metal spatula to racks to cool.

When the cookies are cool, store them in an airtight container.

Black Walnut Pearls

ABOUT 40 COOKIES

Do you know black walnuts? They have a flavor all their own that's different from other walnuts. And do you know Mexican wedding cakes? They are round balls of nutty, buttery, dry, and tender cookies, which—as they say—melt in your mouth. This wonderful recipe is really a Mexican wedding cake made with black walnuts. *Muy bueno.*

8 ounces (2 cups) black walnuts
2 cups sifted unbleached flour
1 teaspoon baking soda
¼ teaspoon salt
6 ounces (1½ sticks) unsalted butter
1 teaspoon vanilla extract
¼ cup granulated sugar
2 tablespoons heavy cream
Confectioners sugar (to sprinkle on the baked cookies)

Adjust a rack one third down from the top of the oven and preheat oven to 325 degrees. Line cookie sheets with baking parchment or aluminum foil, shiny side up.

On a board, with a long, heavy knife, chop the walnuts into medium-small pieces; set aside.

Sift together the flour, baking soda, and salt; set aside.

In the large bowl of an electric mixer beat the butter until soft. Beat in the vanilla, sugar, and cream. On low speed, add the sifted dry ingredients and beat only to mix. Remove the bowl from the mixer and stir in the nuts.

Now, next to the sink, spread out a large piece of aluminum foil. Use a rounded teaspoonful of the dough for each cookie. Place them any which way on the foil. Wet your hands under cold water and, with wet hands roll a mound of the dough into a ball; place it on the lined sheet. Place the balls about 1 inch apart. Wet your hands as often as necessary.

Bake one sheet at a time for about 25 minutes, reversing the sheet front to back once during baking. Bake until the cookies are golden.

The baked cookies may be transferred to a rack to cool or, if you are using a cookie sheet with three flat sides, just slide the paper or foil off the sheet. Let stand for a few minutes, then turn the cookies upside down and let cool all the way.

Place all the cooled cookies, right side up, right next to each other, on a large piece of paper or foil.

Through a fine strainer sprinkle confectioners sugar generously over the cookies.

These are pretty in little fluted paper cups, or pack them as they are in an airtight container.

Peanut Raisin Spice Cookies

26 VERY LARGE COOKIES

Jumbo-sized cookies with a gigantic amount of peanuts and raisins, these are crisp and crunchy and chewy, with a mild flavor of spices. They are great.

3 cups sifted unbleached flour
1 teaspoon baking powder
1 teaspoon baking soda
½ teaspoon salt
1 teaspoon ground ginger
½ teaspoon ground cinnamon
½ teaspoon ground nutmeg
8 ounces (2 sticks) unsalted butter
1 teaspoon vanilla extract
1¾ cups granulated sugar
2 eggs graded "large"
15 ounces (2½ cups) raisins
8 ounces (2 cups) salted peanuts

Adjust two racks to divide the oven into thirds and preheat oven to 350 degrees. Line cookie sheets with baking parchment or with aluminum foil, shiny side up; set aside.

Sift together the flour, baking powder, baking soda, salt, ginger, cinnamon, and nutmeg; set aside.

In the large bowl of an electric mixer beat the butter until soft. Beat in the vanilla and sugar. Add the eggs and beat until mixed. On low speed add about half the sifted dry ingredients and beat until incorporated.

Remove the bowl from the mixer. Stir in the remaining dry ingredients. The mixture will be quite stiff. With a heavy, wooden spatula stir in the raisins and peanuts (it will take a lot of stirring).

You can either shape these with a 2-inch ice cream scoop, a ¼-cup measuring cup, or a large spoon. Place them on the lined sheets about 2½ inches apart (only six on a 17 by 14-inch-sheet). If you have used an ice cream scoop or a measuring cup, flatten the mounds to a ½-inch thickness with the underside of a wet fork. If you have used a spoon to form the mounds, it is best to pick each one up, roll it between your hands into a ball, and then flatten it between your hands to a ½-inch thickness, about 2½ inches in diameter.

Bake two sheets at a time for about 18 minutes, reversing the sheets once or twice top to bottom and front to back. Bake until the cookies are golden brown all over.

If you bake one sheet alone, bake it in the middle of the oven. And watch it, it might be necessary to move it to the top position to help it brown on top.

Remove the cookies with a wide metal spatula and transfer to a rack to cool.

Store in an airtight container.

The $250.00 Cookie Recipe

ABOUT 54 COOKIES—
3 POUNDS

A lady and her daughter had lunch at Neiman-Marcus in Dallas, Texas. For dessert they ordered the "Neiman-Marcus Cookie." It was so delicious that the lady asked the waitress if she could have the recipe.

"I'm afraid not."

"Could I buy the recipe?"

"Yes."

"How much?"

"Two fifty."

The lady was pleased and asked the waitress to just add it to her bill.

A month later when she received her credit card statement she saw, "Cookie recipe—$250.00."

She spoke to the credit department at the store and asked them to take back the recipe and credit her account. The store people said they couldn't do that. They said that all of their recipes were very expensive so that everybody wouldn't get them and copy them.

The lady customer told the store people that she was going to spread the recipe all over the country. The store people said, "We wish you wouldn't do that." But she did. She said it was the only way she could get even.

She sent the recipe to many people. Among them was someone who sent it to someone who sent it to me, with the following note. "Have fun. This is not a joke—this is a true story. Please spread the recipe around to everyone you know."

The day it came in my mail I was very busy, and I had a dinner date that night. But I couldn't sleep until I made it. I made it at midnight. The cookies are delicious.

Here's the recipe. (Spread it around.)

2 cups sifted unbleached flour
1 teaspoon baking powder
1 teaspoon baking soda

½ teaspoon salt
2½ cups old-fashioned (not "instant") oatmeal
4 ounces milk chocolate
8 ounces (2 sticks) unsalted butter
¾ packed cup light brown sugar
½ cup granulated sugar
1 teaspoon vanilla extract
2 eggs graded "large"
12 ounces (2 cups) semisweet chocolate morsels
6 ounces (1½ cups) walnuts, in medium-sized pieces

Adjust two racks to divide the oven into thirds and preheat oven to 375 degrees. Line cookie sheets with baking parchment or aluminum foil, shiny side up; set aside.

Sift together the flour, baking powder, baking soda, and salt; set aside.

Place the oatmeal in the bowl of a food processor fitted with the metal chopping blade. Cut or break the milk chocolate into pieces and add it to the oatmeal. Process for 20 or 25 seconds, until the oatmeal and the chocolate are almost powdered. Set aside.

In the large bowl of an electric mixer beat the butter until soft. Add both sugars and the vanilla, and beat until mixed. Beat in the eggs. Then, add the sifted dry ingredients and the oatmeal mixture and beat on low speed, scraping the bowl with a rubber spatula as necessary and beating only until mixed.

Remove the bowl from the mixer and stir in the chocolate morsels and walnuts. (It will be a stiff mixture.)

Place a long piece of aluminum foil next to the sink. Use a rounded tablespoon of the dough for each cookie. Place mounds of the dough any which way on the foil.

Wet your hands with cold water. Shake them off a bit but don't dry them. Roll a mound of the dough between your hands to form a ball, flatten it a bit, and place it on a lined cookie sheet. Continue shaping the cookies and placing them about 2 inches apart on the lined sheets. Wet your hands again as often as necessary.

Bake two sheets at a time for about 14 minutes, reversing the sheets top to bottom and front to back as necessary during baking to insure even browning.

When the cookies are lightly colored and are just about firm to the touch, remove the sheets from the oven. Let the cookies stand on the sheets briefly, then transfer them with a wide metal spatula to racks to cool.

Store in an airtight container.

Note: At the suggestion of Renée Wolff of Dover, New Jersey (she's the lady who sent me this recipe), I reduced the amounts of both sugars from the original. Now it's worth more, maybe $350.00.

P.S. According to Marian Burros' "Eating Well" column in *The New York Times,* it was not $250.00, it was $2,500.00, and it never happened anyhow. She said, "A call to the representative in the Neiman-Marcus public relations department brought a small laugh and a sigh, along with the assurance that the store had never charged for a recipe supplied to anyone."

Positively-
the-
Absolutely-
Best-
Chocolate-
Chip
Cookies

ABOUT 50
3-INCH COOKIES

This recipe is in my chocolate book.

Recently, a poll taken among food editors at newspapers and magazines found that chocolate chip cookies were the number-one favorite of all homemade cookies in America. (That's not news.)

Well, this recipe is the mother of all chocolate chip cookie recipes.

The following recipe is exactly like the original Toll House recipe. But now, when I make them, I make a few changes. I use 2 teaspoons vanilla instead of 1. And I use 16 ounces of chocolate instead of 12. Also, instead of using morsels, I use semisweet or bittersweet chocolate bars, cut into pieces (see Note, page 100).

DO NOT sift the flour before measuring it! Just stir it a bit to aerate it.

8 ounces (2 sticks) unsalted butter
1 teaspoon salt
1 teaspoon vanilla extract
¾ cup granulated sugar
¾ firmly packed cup light brown sugar
2 eggs graded "large"
2¼ cups <u>unsifted</u> all-purpose flour
1 teaspoon baking soda
1 teaspoon hot water
8 ounces (2 generous cups) walnuts, cut or broken into medium-sized pieces
12 ounces (2 cups) semisweet chocolate morsels

Adjust two racks to divide the oven into thirds and preheat oven to 375 degrees. Line cookie sheets with baking parchment or with aluminum foil, shiny side up.

In the large bowl of an electric mixer beat the butter until soft. Add the salt, vanilla, and both sugars and beat to mix. Add the eggs and beat to mix. On low speed add about half the flour and, scraping the bowl with a rubber spatula, beat until incorporated.

In a small cup stir the baking soda into the hot water, then mix into the dough. Add the remaining flour and beat only until incorporated.

Remove the bowl from the mixer. Stir in the walnuts and the chocolate.

Spread out a large piece of aluminum foil next to the sink. Use a rounded tablespoonful of the dough for each cookie and place the mounds any which way on the foil.

Then wet your hands with cold water, shake off excess, but do not dry your hands. Pick up a mound of dough and roll it between your wet hands into a ball, then press it between your hands to flatten it to about a ½-inch thickness.

Place the cookies on the lined sheets about 2 inches apart.

Bake two sheets at a time, reversing the sheets top to bottom and front to back as necessary to insure even browning. Bake for about 12 minutes, until the cookies are browned all over. (If you bake one sheet alone, bake it on the upper rack.) The cookies must be crisp; do not underbake.

Let the cookies stand for a few seconds, then transfer with a metal spatula to racks to cool.

Store in an airtight container.

Note: If you use 16 ounces of chocolate (see introduction to recipe) you will think it is too much to be incorporated into the dough. Just be patient. It's not too much.

P.S. I was told that this is a big secret. Mrs. Fields refrigerates her chocolate chip cookie dough before shaping and baking. (Actually, Ruth Wakefield, who created this recipe at Toll House, did also.) The dough should be cold when the cookies go into the oven. I tried it. It's great. The cookies have a much nicer and more even golden brown color.

PENNIES FROM HEAVEN

Icebox Cookies

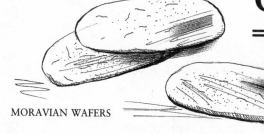

MORAVIAN WAFERS

HEIRLOOM WALNUT
ICEBOX COOKIES

PENNIES FROM HEAVEN
HEIRLOOM WALNUT ICEBOX COOKIES
CHOCOLATE ON PEANUT BUTTER SANDWICHES
MORAVIAN WAFERS
MILK CHOCOLATE AND ALMOND FREEZER COOKIES

Pennies from Heaven

ABOUT 70 SMALL
COOKIE SANDWICHES

Tiny cookie sandwiches, delicate and dainty, with a dough that is a delicious classic shortbread. It is baked in rounds not much larger than quarters, and they are sandwiched together with just a bit of buttercream. Make these for a tea party. Or serve them alongside a fruit or ice cream dessert.

The recipe is from Chris Gargone, the executive pastry chef at Remi, which Gael Greene called the best Italian restaurant in New York City. At Remi they serve these on a plate of assorted cookies. However I serve them, I don't have enough. They are too good.

½ cup old-fashioned oatmeal (to use when shaping the dough into long, thin rolls)
1 cup plus 1 tablespoon sifted unbleached flour
1 cup plus 1 tablespoon strained cornstarch
1 cup plus 1 tablespoon confectioners sugar
8 ounces (2 sticks) unsalted butter
Pinch of salt
1 teaspoon vanilla extract

Place the oatmeal in the bowl of a food processor fitted with the metal chopping blade. Pulse the machine several times, until the oatmeal is powdery. Remove from the processor; set aside.

It is not necessary to wash and dry the processor bowl and blade now.

Place the flour, cornstarch, and sugar in the bowl of the food processor fitted with the metal chopping blade. Pulse once or twice to mix. Cut the butter into ½-inch pieces and add to the flour mixture, along with the salt and vanilla. Process only until the ingredients form a ball and hold together.

Work with half the dough at a time.

Spread the processed oatmeal on a large board or work surface. Place the dough on the oatmeal. With your hands, form the dough into a tube shape. Roll gently, back and forth, using both hands. Start at the center and work your hands out—as you roll—to the ends. Roll until the dough is 11 inches long, about 1¼ inches in diameter, and evenly shaped. Set aside; roll the remaining half of the dough to the same size and shape.

Place the rolls on a cookie sheet (you can just roll them onto it) and refrigerate for about an hour (or longer if you wish).

To bake, adjust a rack in the center of the oven and preheat oven to 325 degrees. Line cookie sheets with baking parchment or aluminum foil, shiny side up.

Use a knife with a very sharp and very thin blade. Cut the dough into slices about ⅛ inch thick or a little thicker. Place the slices ½ to 1 inch apart on the lined sheets.

Bake one sheet at a time for 14 to 16 minutes, until the cookies are sandy-colored around the edges (they can still be pale in the centers). Reverse the sheet front to back once during baking to insure even browning. (If some are done before others, remove them individually.)

Transfer the cookies to a rack to cool or slide the paper or foil off the sheet and let stand until the cookies are cool. You can slice and bake both rolls now or, if you wish, you can wrap and freeze one to bake at some other time.

FILLING
3 ounces (¾ stick) unsalted butter
¼ teaspoon vanilla extract
¼ teaspoon dark rum
2 teaspoons heavy cream
½ cup confectioners sugar

In the small bowl of an electric mixer beat the butter until soft. Beat in the vanilla, rum, and cream. Then beat in the sugar.

When well mixed, transfer to a small bowl for ease in handling.

Place a small dab (a scant ¼ teaspoon) of the filling on the bottom of one cookie. Place another cookie over it, bottoms together, and press gently all around to spread out the filling. There should not be enough to show; it should really just be enough to hold the two cookies together. Continue sandwiching all the cookies.

Place them in the refrigerator briefly, only long enough to harden the filling.

You will probably have leftover filling. It can be saved in the freezer for the next time you make these.

Store in an airtight container.

Note: I want to thank my good friends Nick Malgieri and Richard Sax. Without their help, I couldn't have gotten this recipe.

Heirloom Walnut Icebox Cookies

ABOUT 60 COOKIES

The perfect icebox cookie. Thin, light, delicate, and crisp, with a mildly spiced flavor. After you mix and shape the dough into a loaf, it has to be frozen for about 3 hours—or as much longer as you wish. When it is frozen it slices beautifully.

8 ounces (generous 2 cups) walnuts
2 1/4 cups sifted unbleached flour
1/2 teaspoon salt
1/2 teaspoon baking soda
1 teaspoon ground cinnamon
1 teaspoon ground ginger
1 teaspoon ground nutmeg
1/4 teaspoon ground cloves
1/4 teaspoon ground allspice
8 ounces (2 sticks) unsalted butter
1/2 cup granulated sugar
1/2 packed cup light brown sugar
1 egg graded "large"
2 tablespoons milk

Break the nuts into large pieces; set aside.

Sift together the flour, salt, baking soda, cinnamon, ginger, nutmeg, cloves, and allspice; set aside.

In the large bowl of an electric mixer beat the butter until soft. Add both sugars and beat until thoroughly mixed. Beat in the egg and milk. Add the sifted dry ingredients and beat on low speed until incorporated.

Remove the bowl from the mixer, and with a heavy, wooden spatula, stir in the nuts.

Spread out a piece of wax paper (see Note) about 20 inches long. Spoon out the dough to make a thick strip about 12 inches long in the middle of the paper. Lift the two long sides of the wax paper, bring them together on top of the dough (hold them together, touching the top of the dough) and—with your hands—press on the wax paper to shape the dough into an even loaf about 12 inches long, 3 inches wide, and 1½ inches high with squared ends. Press on the paper to make the loaf as smooth as possible.

Place on a cookie sheet or a tray or anything flat and transfer to the freezer for about 3 hours or as much longer as you wish. (If you plan to leave it in the freezer for more than a few hours, rewrap it in aluminum foil.)

To bake, adjust two racks to divide the oven into thirds. Preheat oven to 375 degrees. Line two large cookie sheets with baking parchment.

Unwrap the loaf, and with a very sharp knife (one with a thin blade, if possible) cut the frozen loaf into slices a scant ¼ inch thick. Place them about 1½ inches apart on the lined sheets.

Bake about 10 minutes, reversing the sheets top to bottom and front to back once or twice during baking. When the cookies are nicely browned and spring back when gently pressed with a fingertip, transfer them with a wide metal spatula to racks to cool.

If you bake 1 sheet alone, bake it in the middle of the oven.

Store in an airtight container.

Note: Because this is a generous amount of dough—and it is quite soft—it is better to wrap it in wax paper than in plastic wrap because wax paper has a little more body.

Chocolate on Peanut Butter Sandwiches

32 COOKIES

These take a little more care and patience than some others, but they are superb. Melted chocolate is sandwiched between the best-ever peanut butter cookies—before baking. During baking the two cookies run together and the chocolate spreads out in a thin layer in the middle. Sensational!

The cookie dough will be shaped like icebox cookies, and then has to be frozen for a few hours or as much longer as you wish before it is sliced (it has to be frozen hard or it will be too soft to slice), sandwiched with the chocolate, and baked.

1¼ cups sifted unbleached flour
½ teaspoon salt
½ teaspoon baking soda
4 ounces (1 stick) unsalted butter
½ cup smooth peanut butter
1 cup granulated sugar
1 egg graded "large"
Scant 1 tablespoon milk

Sift together the flour, salt, and baking soda; set aside.

In the large bowl of an electric mixer beat the butter until soft. Add the peanut butter and sugar and beat well. Add the egg and milk and beat until pale. On low speed add the sifted dry ingredients and beat only until incorporated.

Spread out a piece of plastic wrap about 12 inches long. Spoon half the dough in a strip about 7 or 8 inches long down the middle of the plastic wrap.

Lift the two long sides of the plastic wrap, bring them together on top of the dough, and close them together tightly against the dough. (This will spread and smooth the dough.) Then press on the plastic wrap to form the dough into a sausage shape about 2 inches in diameter. Twist the ends of the plastic wrap to make flat (not pointed) ends on the dough.

Repeat with the remaining dough and another piece of plastic wrap.

Place both pieces of shaped dough in the freezer for a few hours or longer.

FILLING
6 ounces semisweet chocolate (see Note)
2 teaspoons butter

About half an hour before you plan to slice and bake the dough, adjust an oven rack to the middle of the oven (it is best to bake these one sheet at a time) and preheat oven to 375 degrees. Line a large cookie sheet with baking parchment or aluminum foil, shiny side up; set aside.

Break or chop the chocolate into small pieces and place it in the top part of a small double boiler over shallow water on moderate heat. Stir frequently until the chocolate is melted. Add the butter and stir until melted.

Remove the top part of the double boiler and stir frequently to cool. It is best if the chocolate has cooled to room temperature when you use it.

Remove one package of the dough from the freezer and unwrap it. Reserve the other package in the freezer (these can't stand at room temperature for more than a few minutes or the dough becomes too soft to be sliced).

With a fine, sharp knife or a serrated knife, cut a few slices of the dough ¼ inch thick and place each one as you slice it on the lined cookie sheet, about 2 inches apart (these spread). Quickly spoon a scant teaspoonful of the melted and cooled chocolate in the middle of each slice (don't spread it). Again, quickly cut more slices and top each mound of chocolate with a slice. (If some of the chocolate runs out to, or over, the edges, or if it doesn't, it will be OK. But when you place a top cookie over the chocolate, do not press down on it.)

If the dough becomes too soft, rewrap it and return it to the freezer. Unwrap and start to slice the other piece of dough.

Continue slicing the dough and making the sandwiches, returning the dough to the freezer as necessary. If the chocolate hardens while you are working with it, reheat it briefly over hot water as necessary (but if it is too hot it will be too thin and runny).

Bake one sheet at a time for 10 to 12 minutes, until the tops of the cookies are lightly colored all over. Reverse the sheet front to back once during baking to insure even browning (the tops will crack a little—it's OK).

When baked, let the cookies stand on the sheet until they can be transferred easily with a metal spatula; let cool on racks.

Repeat slicing, sandwiching, and baking until all the dough is used.

Store in an airtight container.

Note: There are probably many brands of chocolate that would be as good in this recipe, but although I have made these many times I have only used Lindt "excellence" or Lindt "bittersweet," and they are perfect. Here, in Miami Beach, where I live, Lindt chocolates are available in 3-ounce bars in the candy section of supermarkets.

Moravian Wafers

Moravians are members of a Protestant religious group who settled in Winston-Salem, North Carolina, in 1776. Since then they have been making these special paper-thin spice cookies, especially at Christmas time. They are crisp, brittle, and very peppery-sharp-spicy molasses cookies. Although I bought them for years I never knew, until now, how to make them. They are great!

After you mix and shape the dough into a roll, it must be placed in the freezer for a few hours or overnight (or longer) before you slice and bake the cookies.

One of my favorite restaurants is Mark's Place in North Miami. When I go there for dinner I often bring some of the cookies I baked that afternoon. Mark has had a sampling of many of these cookies. Whichever other cookies I bring, he says, "Don't you have any more Moravian Wafers?"

2 cups sifted unbleached flour
Scant 1/2 teaspoon salt
1 teaspoon baking powder
1/2 teaspoon baking soda
1 1/2 teaspoons ground cinnamon
1 teaspoon ground ginger
1/2 teaspoon ground cloves
1 teaspoon finely ground white pepper (preferably freshly ground)
1/2 teaspoon dry mustard powder
4 ounces (1 stick) unsalted butter
1 cup granulated sugar
1/2 cup mild molasses
1 egg yolk

Sift together the flour, salt, baking powder, baking soda, cinnamon, ginger, cloves, pepper, and mustard; set aside.

In the large bowl of an electric mixer beat the butter until soft. Add the sugar and beat until mixed. Beat in the molasses and egg yolk. On low speed gradually add the sifted dry ingredients and beat until mixed.

Now place a piece of plastic wrap about 18 inches long on the work surface. Spoon the dough down the middle, forming a strip 12 inches long. Lift the two long sides of plastic wrap, bring the sides together on top of the dough, and with your hands, press on the plastic wrap to smooth the dough into an even strip 12 inches long, 2¾ inches wide, and 1¼ inches high with squared ends.

Place the wrapped strip of dough on a cookie sheet and place in the freezer for a few hours, until firm, or as much longer as you wish.

To bake, adjust two racks to divide the oven into thirds and preheat oven to 350 degrees. Line two large cookie sheets with baking parchment or aluminum foil, shiny side up.

Unwrap the strip of dough and place it on a large cutting board. Use a long, sharp knife with a thin blade. Cut the dough into slices ⅛ to ⅒ inch wide. That's very thin (see Note). Place the cookies 1 inch apart on the lined sheets.

Bake two sheets at a time, reversing the sheets top to bottom and front to back once during baking to insure even baking. Bake for 8 to 10 minutes, depending on the thickness of the cookies, until they are lightly colored.

Remove from the oven and let stand for a few minutes until the cookies are cool, then transfer them with a metal spatula.

Store in an airtight container.

Note: With a ruler and the tip of a small, sharp knife, mark the strip in 1-inch lengths. Then slice the strip slowly, carefully, and evenly, and count the slices in each inch. If you get 8 to 10 slices from each inch, you are doing great. Try to cut them the same thinness in order to have them all finish baking at the same time.

Milk Chocolate and Almond Freezer Cookies

ABOUT 72 COOKIES

These are made with both milk chocolate and unsweetened cocoa powder. They are intensely chocolate and deliciously crisp. Unusual and wonderful.

The dough is formed into a loaf shape and then frozen. When you want to bake the cookies, you slice them frozen, then bake.

4 ounces milk chocolate
4 ounces (generous ¾ cup) blanched (skinned) almonds
1 cup granulated sugar
1¾ cups sifted unbleached flour
1 teaspoon baking soda
½ teaspoon baking powder
¼ teaspoon salt
⅓ cup unsweetened cocoa powder (preferably Dutch process)
4 ounces (1 stick) unsalted butter
1 teaspoon vanilla extract
1 egg graded "large"
½ cup apricot preserves

Chop or break up the chocolate and place it and the almonds in the bowl of a food processor fitted with the metal chopping blade. Add half the sugar (reserve remaining sugar) and process for half a minute until the chocolate and nuts are in tiny pieces. Set aside.

Sift together the flour, baking soda, baking powder, salt, and cocoa powder; set aside.

In the large bowl of an electric mixer beat the butter until soft. Add the vanilla and reserved sugar and beat to mix. Beat in the egg and the apricot preserves. Then, on low speed, add the sifted dry ingredients and the processed chocolate-sugar mixture and beat only until incorporated. It will be a stiff mixture; toward the end you will have to stir it by hand.

Spread out two lengths of plastic wrap, each about 13 inches long. Spoon half the dough down the length of each piece of plastic wrap, forming strips about 8 to 9 inches long.

Bring the two long sides of plastic wrap together on top of one strip of dough, pressing them together as close to the dough as possible and smoothing the dough into a strip about 9 inches long, 3 inches wide, and 1 inch high with squared ends. Repeat with the second strip.

Wrap, and freeze for at least 1½ hours, or as much longer as you wish.

To bake, adjust a rack to the center of the oven (it is best to bake these only one sheet at a time) and preheat oven to 350 degrees. Line a cookie sheet with baking parchment or aluminum foil, shiny side up.

Unwrap the frozen dough and, with a sharp knife, cut slices ¼ inch thick. Place them at least 1 inch apart—these spread—on the lined sheet.

These are best when they are baked long enough to be completely crisp, but not longer. You might want to bake a few as a sample to check the timing.

Bake about 11 minutes (they seem to take a bit longer on foil than on parchment). Reverse the sheet front to back once during baking. After 11 minutes they will still feel a bit soft to the touch but they will harden when they cool. Don't let them burn.

When done, let the cookies cool on the sheet for about 2 minutes and then, with a wide metal spatula, transfer to a rack to finish cooling.

Store in an airtight container.

SWEDISH SPICE COOKIES

Rolling Pin Cookies

FRENCH RAISIN
SANDWICH COOKIES

WALNUT HORNS

BROWN SUGAR
TEA COOKIES

CRAIG CLAIBORNE'S CARDAMOM COOKIES
SWEDISH SPICE COOKIES
WHITE PEPPER SHORTBREAD
RUM AND PEPPER GINGERSNAPS
PFEFFERNÜSSE
FRENCH RAISIN SANDWICH COOKIES
FRENCH HONEY WAFERS
PRUNE OR APRICOT HALF-MOONS
SABLÉS
BROWN SUGAR TEA CAKES
WALNUT HORNS
ESPRESSO CHOCOLATE SHORTBREAD

Craig Claiborne's Cardamom Cookies

36 COOKIES

Craig is my hero. Not only is he my all-time favorite cookbook author, but even if he had never written a recipe, I would love him just as much. This delicious cookie is from his book, *An Herb and Spice Cookbook*, which was published in 1963.

Did you ever use cardamom? I did, but I never really tasted it until I tried this recipe. This time, instead of buying ground cardamom, I bought the whole seeds and peeled and ground them myself just before using. There is a big difference in flavor—involved and exotic but mellow.

I have often bought packaged cookies and thought the texture of the cookies divine. I read the ingredients to see if I could find out what was responsible for the texture. The list of ingredients included so many strange names of chemicals that I didn't have a clue as to what had made them so crisp, flaky, sandy, and light. Well, these cookies have that same elusive texture but no strange-sounding ingredients.

These are lovely, simple cookies with an unusual flavor and texture—and once you have prepared the cardamom (it takes a few minutes), they are quick and easy.

A *few teaspoonfuls whole cardamom (to make ½ teaspoon ground)*
2¼ *cups sifted unbleached flour*
1 *teaspoon cream of tartar*
4 *ounces (1 stick) unsalted butter*
1 *teaspoon baking soda*
¼ *teaspoon salt*
1 *packed cup light brown sugar*
1 *egg graded "large"*

Adjust a rack to the middle of the oven and preheat oven to 350 degrees. Line cookie sheets with baking parchment or aluminum foil, shiny side up; set aside.

The cardamom pods may be green or bleached. The green will have a little more flavor than the bleached, but they're both good. To prepare them, work on a cutting board. With a sharp knife cut a few teaspoonfuls of the pods in half the long way. Then either shake the seeds (they will be black and/or gray) out of the shells, or, if necessary, use the point of a small knife to nudge them out. Discard the shells. Grind the seeds in an electric grinder; you could use a coffee grinder or a pepper mill (I use a Cuisinart Mini-Mate). Strain through a fine sieve. Measure ½ teaspoon; set aside.

Sift together the flour and cream of tartar; set aside.

In the small or large bowl of an electric mixer beat the butter until soft. Add the ground cardamom, baking soda, and salt; beat to mix. Beat in the sugar, then the egg. Finally, on low speed, add the sifted dry ingredients and beat until incorporated.

Flour a pastry cloth and a rolling pin. Work with half the dough at a time. Roll out the dough until it is ¼ inch thick. Cut with a round cookie cutter (I use a 2-inch round cutter). Place the cookies 1½ inches apart on the lined sheets.

Bake one sheet at a time for about 10 minutes, reversing the sheet front to back once after 5 minutes. The cookies will rise and puff up during baking, and then they will begin to settle down a bit just when they are done. When done, they will be a light-golden honey color all over.

With a wide metal spatula transfer to racks to cool; when cool, store in an airtight container.

Swedish Spice Cookies

ABOUT 40 3½-INCH
COOKIES

These are elegant—extremely thin and wonderfully crisp and brittle cookies—with a perfectly delicious combination of spices. And the dough is a joy to work with—it's easy to roll very thin. What's more, they are strong enough to be mailed without breaking (I mailed them from Florida to California as a birthday present to Wolfgang Puck).

The dough should be refrigerated for about an hour or so—up to a week if you wish—before it is rolled out, cut into rounds, and baked. If it has been refrigerated for more than an hour, it will be too firm to be rolled out; it should stand at room temperature for half an hour or more, until it can be rolled.

⅔ cup dark corn syrup
½ firmly packed cup light brown sugar
4 ounces (1 stick) unsalted butter
6 ounces (scant 1¼ cups) blanched (skinned) almonds
2 cups sifted unbleached flour
¼ teaspoon baking soda
½ teaspoon ground allspice
2 teaspoons ground ginger
1 teaspoon ground cinnamon
½ teaspoon salt
½ teaspoon black or white pepper, ground fine (preferably freshly
    ground)
1 tablespoon plus 1 teaspoon dark rum, scotch, or brandy
½ teaspoon almond extract
Finely grated rind of 2 large and firm lemons

Place the corn syrup, sugar, and butter in a saucepan with about a 6-cup capacity. Place over moderate heat and stir occasionally until the mixture comes to a boil. Let boil for about 2 minutes. Then set aside to cool a bit.

Toast the almonds in a shallow pan in the middle of a 350-degree oven for about 12 minutes, until the nuts are lightly colored and smell like toasted almonds when you open the oven door. Stir the nuts a few times during toasting so that they brown evenly. Set aside to cool.

Meanwhile, sift together the flour, baking soda, allspice, ginger, cinnamon, salt, and pepper. Set aside.

Remove about 20 of the toasted almonds, place them on a chopping board, and with a long and heavy knife chop into small pieces. Set aside to use as the topping when you bake the cookies.

Place the remaining toasted almonds in the bowl of a food processor fitted with the metal chopping blade. Add about ¼ cup of the sifted dry ingredients and process for about 30 seconds, until fine.

When the corn syrup mixture cools to tepid, add the rum, scotch, or brandy, the almond extract, and the grated rind; stir to mix.

Place the processed nut mixture and the reserved dry ingredients in a large bowl and stir to mix. Then add the corn syrup mixture and stir again to mix.

Spread out three 12-inch lengths of plastic wrap or wax paper, and place about one-third of the mixture on each piece. Fold the sides of the plastic wrap or wax paper over the dough, flatten each piece slightly, and refrigerate for an hour or more.

When you are ready to bake, remove the dough from the refrigerator long enough ahead of time so that it can be rolled out (half an hour or more depending on how long it was refrigerated).

Adjust two racks to divide the oven into thirds and preheat oven to 375 degrees. Line cookie sheets with baking parchment or aluminum foil, shiny side up.

Flour a pastry cloth and a rolling pin. Unwrap one piece of the dough and place it on the floured cloth. If necessary, pound the dough a bit with the rolling pin to soften it. Or let it stand at room temperature until you can roll it. Then, with the floured rolling pin, roll the dough out carefully until it is very thin (a scant ⅛ inch thick) and even all over. During rolling, turn the dough upside down once or twice to flour both sides, and re-flour the cloth and the pin a bit as necessary.

Use a round cookie cutter. I use one that is 3½ inches in diameter, but there is no reason you can't use any other size. (Smaller cookies will bake in less time.) Starting at the outside edge of the dough, cut out the cookies right next to each other. Then, with a metal spatula, transfer the cookies to the lined sheets, placing them 1 inch apart.

Reserve the scraps of dough.

Sprinkle some of the chopped nuts over each cookie. With your fingertips, press the nuts gently into the cookies so that they don't fall off.

Roll and cut the remaining pieces of dough, and sprinkle them with chopped nuts.

After cutting the cookies, press the scraps together, re-roll, and cut.

Bake two sheets at a time, reversing them top to bottom and front to back once during baking. The cookies should bake for 8 to 10 minutes (depending on their thickness). They should be only lightly colored. Do not overbake.

With a wide metal spatula transfer the baked cookies to racks to cool.

When cool, store in an airtight container.

P.S. I go to a juice bar near my home several times a week. (I get a small shot glass of wheat grass juice and a tall chaser of carrot, celery, and beet juice. Not bad.) Danny, the charming young man behind the counter, says he is definitely a cookie man, and he never knew it until he met me. He has had many of the cookies in this book, but these Swedish Spice Cookies are his favorite. Danny is trying to convince me to bake these for the juice bar. They would sell them, and he predicts grand fortunes for all of us. All I would have to do is bake the cookies.

White Pepper Shortbread

16 COOKIES

This is a classic, old-fashioned shortbread with a new flavor and a new shape. The flavor is white pepper—so mild and mellow you won't be sure it tastes like pepper. The shape is similar to the shape of bear's paws (the Danish pastry). They're gorgeous and delicious, and quick and easy.

1¼ cups sifted unbleached flour
¼ cup granulated sugar
½ teaspoon finely ground white pepper
    (preferably freshly ground)
4 ounces (1 stick) cold unsalted butter

Adjust a rack to the center of the oven and preheat oven to 350 degrees. Line a cookie sheet with baking parchment or aluminum foil, shiny side up; set aside.

This can be mixed in a food processor or an electric mixer (or just in a bowl with a big spoon).

In a processor bowl fitted with the metal chopping blade place the flour, sugar, and pepper. Pulse once or twice to mix. On a board, cut the butter the long way into fourths, then cutting through all four strips at once, cut it into small pieces (¼ to ½ inch wide). Add the butter to the bowl and process for about 30 seconds, until the ingredients hold together.

In a mixer first beat the butter, sugar, and pepper until mixed. Then mix in the flour.

Turn the dough out onto a floured pastry cloth and knead it just a bit, until smooth. Form the dough into a square shape about an inch thick.

Roll the dough with a floured rolling pin. While rolling, keep the shape as square as possible and keep the sides as straight as possible. Keep a ruler handy and press it up against the sides often to straighten them. If necessary, re-flour the cloth and the rolling pin a bit while working. Roll the dough evenly in both directions until it is about 8 inches square and a generous ¼ inch thick.

With the ruler and the tip of a small knife, mark the dough into four 2-inch strips in one direction, then in the opposite direction to make 2-inch squares. Place the ruler on top of the dough, and with a small, sharp knife, cutting against the ruler, cut in one direction and then in the opposite direction to make sixteen 2-inch squares.

With a wide metal spatula transfer the squares to the lined cookie sheet.

With the small, sharp knife, cut each cookie in one direction into 4 strips, making each cut about 1¼ inches long; do not cut all the way through to the end.

With the tip of the knife, and/or with your fingers, separate the strips (the bear's paws) about ¼ inch apart at the open end. And keep the cookies at least ½ inch apart from each other.

Bake for 15 to 18 minutes, until lightly colored, reversing the sheet front to back once during baking.

When you remove the sheet from the oven, let the cookies stand on the sheet for about 5 minutes, then transfer with a metal spatula to a rack to cool.

Store in an airtight container.

Rum and Pepper Gingersnaps

SEE NOTE AS TO YIELD

The flavor is exotic, the texture wonderful. These are rolled paper-thin (almost) and, when baked, they have a light, flaky, almost porous texture (although they are very crisp).

Because the dough is rolled so thin, it takes time to roll, cut, and bake it all. You might want to make only a dozen or so at one time and make the rest at some other time. The dough can be wrapped and refrigerated or frozen. (If it is chilled for a long time, it will have to stand at room temperature for a while before it can be rolled out.)

1 cup granulated sugar
4 tablespoons water
2½ tablespoons light molasses
4 ounces (1 stick) unsalted butter
3¾ cups sifted unbleached flour
½ teaspoon salt
1 teaspoon finely and freshly ground black or white pepper
3 teaspoons ground ginger
½ teaspoon ground cloves
1½ teaspoons baking soda
4 tablespoons dark rum or cognac
Finely grated rind of 1 large, firm, and cold lemon

Stir the sugar, water, and molasses in a small saucepan over moderate heat until it just barely begins to bubble. Remove from the heat. Cut the butter into pieces and stir into the hot mixture to melt. Set aside and let cool. (If you wish, transfer the hot butter mixture to a bowl to cool more quickly.)

Meanwhile, sift together into a large bowl the flour, salt, pepper, ginger, and cloves.

When the butter mixture is cool, stir in the baking soda, rum or cognac, and the lemon rind. Then pour this into the sifted dry ingredients and stir until smooth.

The mixture will be too thin to roll out, but just let it stand for a few minutes at room temperature, then chill briefly (10 minutes in the freezer) and it will be fine to roll.

Meanwhile, adjust two racks to divide the oven into thirds and preheat oven to 375 degrees. Line cookie sheets with baking parchment or with aluminum foil, shiny side up. Set aside.

Flour a pastry cloth and rolling pin. Place about 1 cup of the dough on the pastry cloth. Turn it upside down to flour both sides, and roll it out very, very thin. While rolling, turn the dough upside down a few times, and re-flour the cloth and pin as necessary. (To turn it upside down, it is best to roll it up on the rolling pin and then unroll it upside down.) One cup of the dough should roll into a round shape about 18 inches in diameter. It will be about ⅛ inch or less thick.

When it is rolled out, pierce it all over (about ½ inch apart) with the prongs of a dinner fork to prevent bubbles during baking.

Then cut it with any cookie cutter you like. I use a plain, round, 4-inch circle. With a wide metal spatula transfer the cookies to the lined sheets, placing them very close together (the dough shrinks a bit during baking). After you cut all the large rounds, you can use the same cutter to cut half-moon shapes from most of the remaining piece of rolled-out dough. Any leftover scraps can be pressed together and re-rolled.

Bake two sheets at a time. Transfer the sheets top to bottom and front to back once during baking. Bake for about 10 minutes. You must be very careful when timing these. If they bake too long, they will not taste as good. If they don't bake long enough, they will be soft instead of crisp (in which case they can always be put back in the oven for a few minutes). But they must cool before you can tell if they're crisp. If you bake only one sheet at a time, it should be in the center of the oven and it will probably take about 8 minutes.

When done, you can either transfer them with a wide metal spatula to racks to cool or you can just turn them upside down to cool on the paper.

Store in an airtight container.

Note: This makes many cookies—I don't know how many. You will see what I mean.

Pfeffernüsse

Firm cookies with exotic spices. Great! These are German. They are traditional Christmas cookies, but they are delicious any time at all. The name means "pepper-nuts." The ingredients include both pepper and nuts, along with many other spices.

The dough must be chilled in the freezer or refrigerator before it can be rolled out, cut, and baked. If you have a very wide, round cookie cutter, use it to cut these—the bigger the better. The baked cookies will last well for weeks.

½ pound (1⅔ cups) blanched (skinned) hazelnuts or almonds
4 cups sifted unbleached flour
½ teaspoon salt
½ teaspoon finely ground black or white pepper (preferably freshly ground)
1½ teaspoons ground cinnamon
¼ teaspoon ground cloves
1 teaspoon ground ginger
1 teaspoon dry powdered mustard
¼ teaspoon ground mace
¼ teaspoon ground cardamom
10 ounces (2½ sticks) unsalted butter
1¼ packed cups light brown sugar
¾ cup mild honey
⅓ cup warm water
½ teaspoon baking soda

First toast the nuts in a shallow pan in the middle of a 350-degree oven for about 10 minutes, until they are only lightly toasted. Cool the nuts.

Place the nuts and ¼ cup of the flour (reserve the remaining 3¾ cups flour) in the bowl of a food processor fitted with a metal chopping blade. Pulse the machine three or four times until the nuts are chopped medium-fine. Then process for about 5 seconds until the nuts are in pieces about the size of grains of uncooked rice. Set aside.

Sift together the reserved 3¾ cups flour with the salt, pepper, cinnamon, cloves, ginger, mustard, mace, and cardamom; set aside.

In the large bowl of an electric mixer beat the butter until soft. Add the sugar and beat until thoroughly mixed. Beat in the honey. Reserve about 2 tablespoons of the water and add the rest to the mixing bowl, beating to mix. It will look curdled, but it's OK.

In a small cup stir the reserved 2 tablespoons water with the baking soda until the soda is dissolved; add to the bowl and mix.

Then, on low speed gradually beat in the sifted dry ingredients. Finally, beat in the chopped nuts.

Spread out three large pieces of plastic wrap or wax paper. Divide the dough onto the plastic wrap or paper, wrap, and then flatten each package to about a 1-inch thickness.

Place the packages in the freezer for about 1 hour (no longer) or in the refrigerator for at least 3 hours (or as much longer as you wish).

To bake, adjust two racks to divide the oven in thirds and preheat oven to 350 degrees. Line cookie sheets with baking parchment or aluminum foil, shiny side up, and set aside.

Flour a pastry cloth and a rolling pin. Unwrap a piece of the dough. Cut it in half. Work with one half, rewrapping the other half and placing it in the refrigerator until you are ready to use it.

Place the dough on the floured cloth. If it is very firm pound it a bit with the rolling pin. Turn the dough upside down occasionally while you work with it, and re-flour the pastry cloth and the rolling pin as necessary. Roll out the dough to a ¼-inch thickness.

Using a large, round cookie cutter (mine is 3½ inches in diameter), start to cut the cookies on the outer edge (not in the middle) of the dough, and cut them touching each other.

Place the cookies about an inch apart on the lined sheets. It might be necessary to use a metal spatula to transfer the cookies from the pastry cloth to the sheets.

Use a smaller cutter to cut cookies from any of the scraps that are large enough. Press any other scraps together, re-wrap, and re-chill.

Bake for about 18 minutes, reversing the sheets top to bottom and front to back once during baking. Bake until the cookies are golden.

If the cookies on the lower rack start to darken too much around the edges, slide another cookie sheet under them—the double sheet will protect the bottoms.

Cool briefly on the sheets until the cookies are firm enough to be moved.

With a wide metal spatula transfer the cookies to racks to cool.

Store in an airtight container.

French
Raisin
Sandwich
Cookies

24 COOKIES

These are from Paris. The cookies are hard/ dry/plain, with a layer of raisins in the middle. They are not rich or sweet or fancy. They are perfectly plain, perfect with tea or coffee, even delicious for breakfast or at midnight with a glass of milk. These keep well and they are easy to pack and mail or pack for a lunchbox or a picnic.

There are two waiting periods before the cookies are baked. After the dough is mixed, it is refrigerated for about an hour and then is rolled out on a pastry cloth with a rolling pin and sandwiched with raisins. Then it has to be frozen for several hours or overnight before it is cut into bars and baked.

2 cups sifted unbleached flour
$^{1}/_{2}$ teaspoon baking powder
$^{1}/_{8}$ teaspoon salt
$1^{1}/_{2}$ ounces (3 tablespoons) unsalted butter
$^{1}/_{3}$ cup granulated sugar
7 tablespoons milk
8 ounces (generous $1^{1}/_{2}$ cups) raisins

Sift together the flour, baking powder, and salt; let stand. In the small bowl of an electric mixer beat the butter and sugar to mix. Add the sifted dry ingredients in three additions alternately with the milk in two additions, and beat until mixed.

Lightly flour a work surface and your hands. Turn the dough out onto the floured surface, form it into a mound, and turn it from side to side to flour it all over. Form it into an even oblong 3 by 6 inches with square corners and about 1¼ inches thick.

Wrap in plastic wrap and refrigerate for about an hour.

Flour a pastry cloth and a rolling pin. Cut the chilled dough into two 3-inch squares. Return one piece to the refrigerator. On the pastry cloth roll out the other piece of dough neatly and carefully into a 9-inch square, keeping the shape as even as possible. Turn the dough upside down a few times while rolling to keep both sides floured. Reflour the cloth and pin as necessary.

Line a cookie sheet with baking parchment or wax paper. Roll the dough up on the rolling pin and unroll it onto the lined sheet.

Sprinkle the raisins evenly all over the dough (place them carefully all the way to the edges); set aside.

Now roll out the second piece of dough to the same size as the first. Roll it up on the rolling pin and unroll it carefully over the raisins.

Now, carefully, with the rolling pin, roll all over the cake to press it securely together and to roll it out to a 10-inch square. (The raisins will almost come through the top layer of dough.)

Use a ruler to press against the edges of the dough, making them straight and even. As you press the edges with the ruler, with your other hand press the dough out to reach the ruler wherever necessary. (You can make the edges quite straight this way.)

Now place the whole thing in the freezer for several hours or cover it with plastic wrap and freeze overnight. If it is really frozen firm, it will be easy to cut neat and perfect oblongs.

Adjust a rack to the middle of the oven and preheat oven to 375 degrees. Line a cookie sheet with baking parchment.

With a long, heavy, sharp knife cut the frozen cake into quarters. Then cut one quarter into three slices, and cut the three slices cross-wise to make six bars. Repeat with all the quarters. Press down firmly on the tops with your hands to secure.

With a metal spatula transfer the bars to the lined cookie sheets.

TOPPING
2 teaspoons milk
1 tablespoon granulated sugar

In a small cup stir the milk and sugar and, with a brush, brush the mixture all over the tops of the cookies.

Bake for 30 to 35 minutes, only until barely golden-colored on top, with slightly darker edges. Do not overbake. Reverse the pan front to back once or twice during baking to insure even browning. During baking, if some of the cookies on the edge of the sheet start to brown faster than those in the middle, use a metal spatula to switch them around, moving those in the middle to the edge and vice versa.

Cool on a rack, then store in an airtight container.

French Honey Wafers

THE YIELD DEPENDS
ON HOW THIN YOU
ROLL THE DOUGH.

Mildly spiced, dry, thin, crisp, crunchy—I love them. It will be necessary to chill the dough for a few hours before rolling, cutting, and baking. I have always been fascinated with any and all extra-thin cookies and crackers. I've made almost every recipe I've seen for thin, thin cookies. This dough is a special joy to work with, but you must work quickly before the dough softens too much.

2 cups sifted unbleached flour
½ teaspoon salt
½ teaspoon baking soda
1 teaspoon ground ginger
½ teaspoon ground cinnamon
½ teaspoon ground nutmeg
4 ounces (1 stick) unsalted butter
⅓ packed cup light brown sugar
⅔ cup light and mild honey

Sift together the flour, salt, baking soda, ginger, cinnamon, and nutmeg; set aside.

In the large bowl of an electric mixer beat the butter until soft. Beat in the sugar and then the honey. On low speed gradually add the sifted dry ingredients and beat until incorporated.

Divide the dough in two and wrap each piece in wax paper or aluminum foil. Refrigerate until firm or longer if you wish.

To bake, adjust two racks to divide the oven into thirds and preheat oven to 350 degrees. Line cookie sheets with baking parchment or aluminum foil, shiny side up. Set aside.

Flour a pastry cloth and rolling pin. Unwrap one package of the dough, and cut it in half. Return one part to the refrigerator and place the other on the pastry cloth.

Work quickly—this dough softens quickly at room temperature.

With the floured rolling pin, roll out the dough to a ⅛-inch thinness, turning the dough upside down a few times while rolling to keep both sides floured.

Cut the cookies with a floured cookie cutter (I use very large, plain shapes—rounds or ovals). Always cut around the outside of the dough first, not in the middle. Before the cookies soften, transfer them with a wide metal spatula to the prepared sheets, placing them about an inch apart. Press together, chill, and re-roll scraps.

Bake two sheets at a time for about 10 to 12 minutes (more or less depending on the thickness). Transfer the sheets top to bottom and front to back once during baking. Bake until a beautiful, light golden-honey color (all cookies should bake as beautifully as these do).

Remove the sheets from the oven. It will probably be necessary to wait a bit for the cookies to firm up before transferring them with a wide metal spatula to racks to cool.

As soon as they cool, store them in an airtight container. Do not let them stand around uncovered.

Prune or Apricot Half-Moons

ABOUT 16 HALF-MOONS

These are not typical cookies. They are small, and they are finger food, but they don't last as long as cookies do. They are best when they are fresh, but you can freeze them and then just heat them a bit before serving; they will be just as good. Wonderful at a tea party, or for breakfast or brunch. They are simple looking—classy and elegant.

If you are handy, you will love making these.

You will make sensational pastry similar to pie crust, chill it a few hours or overnight (or longer), roll it out thin, cut it into rounds, place a dried prune or apricot on each round, fold the pastry like a book over the fruit, brush the tops with egg wash, sprinkle with crystal sugar, and bake.

You will need a round cookie cutter about 3 inches in diameter.

4 ounces (1 stick) cold and firm unsalted butter
1 egg yolk
Ice water
1 cup plus 2 tablespoons sifted unbleached flour
1 tablespoon granulated sugar
¼ teaspoon salt
Small dried pitted prunes and/or apricot halves (Although dried they should be soft, not hard.)

Cut the butter lengthwise into quarters. Cut the pieces—all together—into ¼- to ½-inch slices. Refrigerate.

In a small cup stir the yolk with a fork to mix. Measure the yolk and add ice water to make a total of 3 tablespoons. Stir to mix, then refrigerate.

Place the flour, sugar, and salt in the bowl of a food processor fitted with the metal chopping blade. Pulse the machine once or twice to mix. Add the cold butter and pulse the machine 5 times—no more. Then, with the motor running, add the cold egg yolk mixture through the feed tube and process for only 7 or 8 seconds. Do not process until the ingredients hold together.

Place a length of plastic wrap on the work surface. Turn the ingredients out onto the plastic wrap. Close the plastic wrap over the ingredients and press the mixture together until it holds together and forms a ball. (You should see little pieces of butter in the dough—that's what makes it flaky.) Flatten slightly and refrigerate for a few hours or longer (overnight or for a few days if you wish).

Before you are ready to bake, shape the prunes and/or apricots into ovals—just press the prunes with your fingers into oval shapes and press the apricot halves in half.

Line a large cookie sheet with baking parchment (parchment is better than foil for these).

Flour a pastry cloth and a rolling pin.

Unwrap the dough and cut in half, replacing one piece in the refrigerator while you roll the other. If it is too firm to be rolled out, pound it with the rolling pin until it is soft enough (turn it upside down once during pounding). Roll it out until it is ⅛ inch thick (turn it upside down once during rolling).

Cut only 1 round first as a sample for the size (the size of the cutter will depend on the size of the fruit). Use a plain or scalloped cutter about 3 inches in diameter. (Always start cutting around the outer edges first.)

Place a piece of the shaped fruit on the right side of the round. Brush a little water around the edges of the round. Pick it up with a spatula, place it in your left hand, fold the left side over, and press the edges together to seal. (There must be enough border to press together. If necessary, use a larger cookie cutter or cut the fruit a little smaller.)

Place the half-moon on the lined sheet. Continue to make the remaining half-moons and place them 1 inch apart on the sheet. (Leftover scraps can be re-rolled once or twice.)

Refrigerate the shaped half-moons for 10 minutes (or much longer if you wish, even overnight) before baking.

TOPPING
1 egg yolk
1 teaspoon milk
Crystal sugar (see page 5)

Adjust a rack to the center of the oven and preheat oven to 400 degrees.

In a small cup stir the yolk and milk to mix. Brush the egg wash on the tops of the half-moons and sprinkle them with crystal sugar.

Bake at 400 degrees for 7 minutes. Then reverse the sheet front to back, reduce the temperature to 350 degrees, and continue to bake for 7 to 8 minutes longer (total baking time is 14 to 15 minutes), until the half-moons are golden brown on the tips and just a pale color on the tops. The bottoms will be richly browned.

With a wide metal spatula transfer to a rack to cool.

Serve the same day if possible, or freeze in an airtight freezer box. To serve after freezing, preheat oven to 450 degrees. Wrap as many of the frozen half-moons as you want in a single layer in aluminum foil. Bake for 7 minutes, then turn the oven heat off. Open the foil and return the half-moons, uncovered, to the oven for just 2 or 3 minutes, watching carefully to prevent burning. Cool on a rack.

Sablés

These are special. They are classic traditional French butter cookies made with the hard-boiled yolks of eggs. Elegant enough for a formal dinner, they are also simple and casual and plain. They have a delicious, sandy texture—*sablé* is French for sand—and a hint of lemon flavor. They are fragile and must be handled with care.

2 egg yolks
3 ounces (¾ stick) unsalted butter
Finely grated rind of 1 large, cold, firm lemon
¼ cup granulated sugar
1 cup plus 2 tablespoons sifted unbleached flour
¼ teaspoon salt

Use cookie sheets with only one raised rim or any other sheets upside down. Line cookie sheets with baking parchment or with aluminum foil, shiny side up. Set aside.

To hard-boil the yolks place them in a small pan of water just deep enough to cover them. Place over moderate heat, bring to a simmer, let cook for 2 minutes, then remove from the heat. Let stand for a minute. Then remove the yolks with a slotted spoon and set aside to cool.

When the yolks are cool, place them in the bowl of a food processor fitted with the metal chopping blade. Cut the butter into ½-inch slices and add to the yolks. Process for 5 to 10 seconds, scraping the sides if necessary, until smooth. Then add the lemon rind, sugar, flour, and salt, and process for 15 to 20 seconds, until the ingredients hold together and form a ball.

Turn the dough out onto a floured pastry cloth, and with floured hands, form it into a firm, square shape. With a floured rolling pin very gently roll out the dough until it is about 10 inches square. Keep the shape as square as you can, and keep the sides as straight as you can. It will be only about ⅛ inch thick. Re-flour as necessary.

To straighten the sides, press a ruler or a long, narrow metal spatula against them. (It's OK if they are not perfectly straight.)

With a long-bladed sharp knife—or with a pizza wheel—cut in one direction into 4 equal strips, then cut in the opposite direction into fourths, making 16 squares. Cut each square on an angle, making 32 triangles.

With a metal spatula transfer the triangles to cookie sheets, placing them slightly apart.

Dip a fork in flour and with the underside of the prongs mark a ridged design in any direction on top of each cookie (pressing the fork just once onto each cookie). Re-flour the fork as necessary.

Let the cookies stand on the sheets for 30 minutes to 1 hour.

Meanwhile, adjust two racks to divide the oven into thirds and preheat oven to 350 degrees.

Bake two sheets together for about 15 minutes, until only sandy-colored. Reverse the sheets top to bottom and front to back once during baking to insure even browning.

Slide the parchment or foil off the sheets and let the cookies stand until almost cool. Then, with a metal spatula, turn them upside down (or place them on a rack) and let stand until completely cool.

Store carefully in an airtight container.

P.S. Thanks, Nancy Nicholas. You were responsible for these. They're great!

Brown Sugar Tea Cakes

ABOUT 52
3½-INCH COOKIES

Old-fashioned Southern cookies. Hard, dry, crisp, crunchy, and plain. Sensational. Old-timers say that these get better after you store them for a week. I've never kept them long enough to find out. They are perfect cookie-jar cookies. And, if you wish, they can be cut into fancy shapes. They are also wonderful to hang on a Christmas tree. (Make a small hole in each cookie before baking, and pull a ribbon through it after baking. Bake one as a test to be sure the hole is large enough so that it doesn't close during baking.)

1 tablespoon milk or light cream
Finely grated rind of 2 or 3 large firm lemons
2 tablespoons and 1 teaspoon lemon juice
6 ounces (1½ sticks) unsalted butter
½ teaspoon vanilla extract
1 teaspoon salt
2 firmly packed cups light brown sugar
2 eggs graded "large"
1¾ teaspoons baking soda
5½ cups sifted unbleached flour

Adjust two racks to divide the oven into thirds and preheat oven to 350 degrees. Line cookie sheets with baking parchment or with aluminum foil, shiny side up; set aside.

Place the milk or cream in a 2-cup glass measuring cup (or any bowl at least that size). Stir in the lemon rind and juice; let stand.

In the large bowl of an electric mixer beat the butter, vanilla, and salt. Add the sugar and beat until mixed. Beat in the eggs.

Stir the baking soda into the milk or cream mixture (it will foam up high), then add to the butter and sugar mixture, beating to mix (it will look curdled—it's OK).

On low speed gradually mix in the flour, adding only 1 cup at a time.

When the mixture becomes too stiff for you to continue beating, turn it out onto a large work surface. Add the remaining flour, and knead together with your hands until all the flour is incorporated and the mixture is smooth.

Lightly flour a large pastry cloth and a rolling pin. Work with about one-third of the dough at a time. Roll the dough out until it is about 1/8 inch thick. Use any cookie cutter (I use a 3 1/2-inch scalloped round cutter and the cookies are gorgeous).

Start cutting the cookies around the outside of the rolled-out dough (not in the center), and cut them very close to each other. With a wide metal spatula transfer the cookies to the lined sheets, placing them about 1 inch apart (these will barely spread during baking).

Reserve all scraps of dough, knead them together, re-roll, and recut them.

Bake two sheets at a time for about 15 minutes, until the cookies are golden-colored. During baking reverse the sheets top to bottom and front to back once to insure even browning.

With a wide metal spatula transfer the baked cookies to racks to cool. Then store in an airtight container.

Note: I have also rolled these to about half the thickness mentioned above. They baked in about 10 minutes or less. They were wonderful. Try a few rolled really thin and see what you think.

Walnut Horns

(a.k.a. Rugelach)

64 SMALL HORNS

I had never before made a pastry dough like this one; this calls for melting the butter and then just pouring it in. It's easy as well as delicious and flaky—a joy.

These are small, delicate, and dainty—perfect for a ladies' tea or a luncheon (although I know a tall and tough young man who gobbles them like popcorn).

These are best when they're fresh, but they freeze well.

The dough should be made a day or at least several hours beforehand. With the dough in the refrigerator—or the freezer—you can shape and bake one-fourth or more of them at a time if you don't want them all at once. If the dough has been frozen, plan to let it thaw at room temperature for a few hours or overnight in the refrigerator.

PASTRY DOUGH

8 ounces (2 sticks) unsalted butter
1 egg yolk (reserve the white to use as topping)
1/2 teaspoon salt
1 cup sour cream
Finely grated rind of 2 cold and firm lemons
2 cups sifted unbleached flour

Place the butter in a small saucepan over moderate heat to melt it, then set aside.

In the large bowl of an electric mixer beat the egg yolk, salt, cream, and grated lemon rind to mix. Add the melted butter (which may still be warm or even hot) and the flour and beat to mix, scraping the bowl as necessary with a rubber spatula.

The mixture will appear uneven (it will look curdled). Just place the bowl in the refrigerator for about 10 minutes and stir to mix once or twice. Now it will become smooth.

Place four pieces of plastic wrap or wax paper on a work surface, and place one-fourth of the dough on each piece. Bring up the sides of each piece of plastic wrap or wax paper and form balls of the dough, then flatten them slightly. Wrap the balls of dough and refrigerate overnight. Or, to save time, place them in the freezer for about half an hour, then in the refrigerator for about an hour.

FILLING
8 ounces (2¼ cups) walnuts
¾ cup granulated sugar
2 teaspoons cinnamon
1 teaspoon unsweetened cocoa powder
¼ teaspoon ground nutmeg
¼ teaspoon ground ginger

The walnuts should be cut into small pieces. If you do it in a processor or on a board with a long knife, some pieces will be rather coarse and some will be powdery. In order to get the pieces close in size, I cut them one at a time with a small paring knife. (But I'm a Virgo. I suspect that however you do it, it will be OK.) Set aside.

In a small bowl mix the sugar, cinnamon, cocoa, nutmeg, and ginger; set aside. (Do not mix the nuts into the sugar mixture.)

When you are ready to shape and bake these, adjust an oven rack to the center of the oven and preheat oven to 350 degrees. Line a cookie sheet with baking parchment or aluminum foil, shiny side up.

Flour a pastry cloth and a rolling pin.

Place one ball of the dough on the cloth, and with the rolling pin pound it firmly to soften it a bit. Roll out the dough (turning it over occasionally) to a 12-inch circle.

Sprinkle with one-fourth (about 3 tablespoons) of the sugar mixture. Then sprinkle with one-fourth (a generous ½ cup) of the walnuts, keeping the nuts away from the center of the circle. (Leave about 6 empty inches in the middle. Any nuts in the middle would fall out when you roll up the dough.)

With a rolling pin, roll over the filling to press the ingredients slightly into the dough.

To cut the circle into 16 wedges, you can use a long-bladed knife (this is the easiest) or a pastry wheel that cuts in a small zigzag pattern (this looks very nice). Do it either way.

Roll each wedge jelly-roll fashion, rolling from the outside toward the point. Place the little rolls, points down, 1 inch apart on the lined cookie sheet.

If you are going to bake more than one circle of dough right now (the others can wait if you wish), clean and re-flour the pastry cloth after preparing each circle.

GLAZE
1 egg white
Optional—crystal sugar (see page 5)

In a small bowl beat the egg white just until foamy but not stiff. With a pastry brush, brush it over the tops of the horns.

Sprinkle with the optional crystal sugar.

Bake one sheet at a time for about 25 minutes, until lightly browned, reversing the sheet front to back once during baking to insure even browning. (Some of the sugar mixture will melt and run out during baking.)

Remove from the oven, and with a wide metal spatula transfer the horns to a rack to cool. When cool, store in an airtight container.

Note: While making these, leftover egg white should be beaten again when you need it, just until foamy. It can be saved for a day or two in the refrigerator.

Espresso Chocolate Shortbread

ABOUT 40 COOKIES

This is adapted from the chocolate short-bread recipe in my chocolate book. But now, before baking, the cookies are sprinkled with ground espresso beans. These are sophisticated, exotic, and seductive. Smooth bittersweet chocolate—with the crackle and crunch of espresso beans. Many bakeries around the country have told me that they make this chocolate shortbread (the original way, without the espresso) and that it is one of their most popular cookies.

(It is best if you have wonderful espresso beans and a coffee grinder. I use Starbucks coffee from Seattle.) The coffee must be ground not too coarse and not too fine, but just right. And it is important to sprinkle on not too much of it, and not too little.

2 cups sifted unbleached flour
$\frac{1}{2}$ cup strained unsweetened cocoa powder (preferably Dutch process)
1 cup confectioners sugar
8 ounces (2 sticks) unsalted butter
Espresso beans
Water

Adjust two racks to divide the oven into thirds and preheat oven to 300 degrees. Line cookie sheets with baking parchment or aluminum foil, shiny side up.

This dough can be made in a food processor or in an electric mixer.

To use a processor, fit it with the metal chopping blade and place the flour, cocoa, and sugar in the bowl. Cut the butter in $\frac{1}{2}$-inch slices over the dry ingredients and process until the dough is smooth and holds together.

To use an electric mixer, place the butter in the large bowl of an electric mixer and beat until soft. Add the sugar and beat to mix. Then add the flour and cocoa and beat until the dough holds together and is smooth.

Remove the dough from the bowl, form it into a ball, and flatten it slightly.

Flour a pastry cloth, rubbing the flour in well, and a rolling pin. Place the dough on the cloth and turn it over to flour both sides.

With the floured rolling pin (re-flour it as necessary), roll the dough until it is ½ inch thick (no thinner). Make the thickness as even as possible all over.

Use a plain round cookie cutter preferably 1½ inches in diameter. Before cutting each cookie, dip the cutter in flour and tap it to shake off excess. Start cutting the cookies around the outer edge, not in the middle. Cut them as close to each other as possible. Place the cookies 1 inch apart on the cookie sheets.

Press together leftover scraps of dough, re-flour the cloth as necessary, re-roll the dough, and cut.

Grind a few large spoonfuls of espresso beans in a coffee grinder until a medium grind—not coarse and not fine.

Place a small cup of water next to you. Dip your fingertip in the water, and with your fingertip wet the tops of a few cookies. Carefully sprinkle some of the ground espresso on the wet cookies. I use about ¼ teaspoonful for three cookies, covering only about half of the top of each cookie. Continue wetting a few at a time, and sprinkling them. Then, with a dry fingertip, press gently on the espresso on top of the cookies to press it into the dough a bit (just to prevent it from falling off too easily).

Bake two sheets at a time for 25 to 30 minutes, reversing the sheets top to bottom and front to back once during baking to insure even baking. (If you bake only one sheet at a time, bake it in the middle of the oven.) Watch these carefully—unless you check them often, they could burn and become bitter before you know it.

With a wide metal spatula transfer to a rack to cool.

Store in an airtight container.

CORNMEAL SHORTBREAD FINGERS

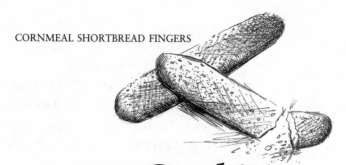

Cookies
Shaped
by Hand
or with a
Pastry Bag or
Cookie Press

SWEET PRETZELS

CHINESE FORTUNE COOKIES

CHINESE FORTUNE COOKIES
SWEET PRETZELS
CORNMEAL SHORTBREAD FINGERS
MUCHO-MACHO SPICE BARS
BITTERSWEET CHOCOLATE MACAROONS
GRAMMIE RAICHLEN'S RIBBON COOKIES
BAGUETTES
CHOCOLATE O'S

Chinese Fortune Cookies

Homemade fortune cookies? Yes, you can make them—and they will be perfectly gorgeous!

Think of the fun you can have writing your own fortunes and placing them in your own fortune cookies. These are designer fortune cookies that look and taste better than the ones you get with chop suey. One year I used them as Christmas cards, with the slip of paper inside that traditionally tells your fortune a Christmas greeting instead. I put each cookie in a small, fancy, cellophane bag (I buy beautiful ones in several party stores and/or paper supply stores). For mailing, I placed each one in a small box filled with popcorn. None of them broke.

These are quick and easy to mix and bake, but (unless you have someone to help you shape them) you will bake and shape only one at a time (with someone to help, you can bake two on a cookie sheet).

Before you start to make the cookies, write or type the fortunes or greetings on strips of paper about 4 inches long and ½ inch wide (see Note).

1 egg white graded "large"
⅛ teaspoon vanilla extract
¼ cup sifted unbleached flour
⅛ teaspoon salt
¼ cup granulated sugar

Adjust a rack one-third up from the bottom of the oven and preheat oven to 400 degrees. Butter a circle about 5 inches in diameter on the middle of the cookie sheet. You will need something to shape the cookies on after they are folded in half; I use the rim of a Pyrex measuring cup.

Cookies Shaped by Hand or with a Pastry Bag or Cookie Press • 201

In a small bowl beat the egg white and vanilla until foamy. Add the flour, salt, and sugar and beat until smooth. Transfer to a small, shallow cup for ease in handling.

Place a teaspoonful (use a regular teaspoon, not a measuring spoon) of the batter in the middle of the buttered section. Tilt the sheet on a sharp angle in all directions to encourage the batter to run out into a round shape about 3 inches in diameter. Keep the shape as round as possible; take your time, be patient. Use the tip of a small paring knife to guide the batter. If one area is thicker than the rest, level it by tilting the cookie sheet.

Bake for about 5 minutes, until the cookie has a golden rim almost ½ inch wide; the cookie will remain pale in the center.

As soon as it is baked you have to work quickly. Place the cookie sheet on a large board (or next to a board). With a wide metal spatula quickly remove the baked cookie and turn it upside down on the board. Quickly place the fortune on the cookie close to the middle, then immediately fold the cookie in half (the fortune goes along the length of the fold on one side of the fold) and quickly place the folded edge of the cookie across the rim of a measuring cup, pulling the pointed ends down, one on the inside and one on the outside of the cup. Hold it there for a few seconds until it becomes crisp.

(About now you might be saying, "Ow—that's hot!" If you wish, wear thin gloves.)

If you work with two cookie sheets, you can be shaping the next cookie while the first is baking. Each cookie sheet has to be washed, dried, and buttered each time. (I tried a nonstick sheet and the cookie didn't hold its shape.)

Continue to bake and shape the cookies. Any time you want to stop, just cover the batter and let it wait at room temperature for a few hours or overnight.

Store these in an airtight container.

Note: To make especially chic and classy fortune cookies use more batter for each one and shape them into a larger size (even 5 to 6 inches in diameter). Use a variety of brightly colored papers for the fortunes, and cut the papers long enough so that they extend out further from the cookies. And cut the ends of the papers into a deep V, or fringe them.

Sweet Pretzels

12 COOKIES

I have always been fascinated with making cookies shaped like pretzels. I've made them from dozens of recipes. None were as good as these. If you like to do things with your hands—things like twisting pretzels—you will be wild about this recipe. The dough is a joy to work with. The pretzels look divine and taste wonderful. They are sensational hanging on a Christmas tree, and are a terrific gift.

There are many superstitions about pretzels. People wore pretzels around their necks to ward off evil spirits (I'm wearing one now on a black velvet ribbon). And pretzels were hung on trees in the belief that they would cause the trees to bear an abundant crop. The shape, which represents your arms crossed over your chest, is said to have been created by a monk in Germany. The pretzels were given to children when they learned their prayers.

The mixed dough should stand for an hour before you shape the pretzels.

2 cups minus 1 tablespoon sifted unbleached flour
Pinch of salt
Optional—¼ teaspoon black or white pepper, finely ground
3 tablespoons granulated sugar
3½ ounces (7 tablespoons) unsalted butter cut in pieces
Finely grated rind of 1 or 2 large, cold, firm lemons
1 egg plus 1 yolk graded "large"

The dough can be mixed in a food processor or with an electric mixer.

In a processor, put everything in the bowl of the processor, which has been fitted with the metal chopping blade, and simply process for about 40 seconds, until the ingredients come together and form a ball. Then knead a bit on a smooth surface.

In a mixer, first beat the butter and sugar to mix. Then add the remaining ingredients and beat, scraping the bowl as necessary, until the ingredients come together. Then knead a bit on a smooth surface.

It will be a stiff dough.

Form it into a tube shape about 8 inches long with flat ends. Wrap airtight in plastic wrap and let stand at room temperature for about an hour.

Before baking, adjust two racks to divide the oven into thirds and preheat oven to 350 degrees. Line cookie sheets with baking parchment or with aluminum foil, shiny side up; set aside.

Cut the roll of dough into 12 even pieces. Cover them loosely with plastic wrap so they don't dry out.

Press one piece of dough into a rough oval. Put it on a lightly floured board. Place your hands on top, with your fingers spread. Work slowly and gently, starting at the middle, and working your hands out to the ends. With your palms and fingers roll the dough back and forth to elongate it. Do this a few times, until the dough is 10½ to 11 inches long, a bit wider in the middle, and slightly tapered at the ends. Reflour the board and your fingers very lightly, as necessary.

Working on the board, shape a pretzel. Cross the two ends about 1½ inches from the ends and then bring them to the other side, forming a simple pretzel shape. With a brush, dab a bit of water under the ends where they cross the other side of the pretzel.

With a metal spatula transfer to a lined cookie sheet. Continue shaping the cookies and placing them an inch or two apart.

TOPPING
1 egg yolk
½ teaspoon water
Crystal sugar (see page 5)

In a small cup mix the egg yolk and water.

Brush a few pretzels with two coats of the egg wash, and sprinkle them generously with the crystal sugar. Continue to glaze and sugar all of the cookies, a few at a time.

Bake two sheets together for about 30 minutes, reversing the sheets top to bottom and front to back once during baking.

When the pretzels are a beautiful pale golden color, and gorgeous, transfer them with a metal spatula to a rack to cool. Store in an air-tight container.

Note: If you don't have crystal sugar, just use the egg wash (it will give the pretzels a nice shiny color), and even with no sugar topping they will still look great.

Cornmeal Shortbread Fingers

Don't even *think* ladyfingers; these are hard, dry, and crunchy. They are extraordinary. Great with tea or coffee—even with wine— or just to nibble on anytime. They are shaped with a pastry bag and a plain round tube.

ABOUT 40 COOKIES

7 ounces ($1^3/_4$ sticks) unsalted butter
$^1/_2$ teaspoon vanilla extract
Generous $^1/_4$ teaspoon finely ground
    white pepper (preferably freshly
    ground)
$^1/_4$ teaspoon salt
$^3/_4$ cup granulated sugar
2 eggs plus 1 additional egg white graded
    "large"
$1^3/_4$ cups sifted unbleached flour
$^2/_3$ cup plus 1 tablespoon cornmeal
    (see Note)
Finely grated rind of 2 large and firm
    lemons

Adjust two racks to divide the oven into thirds and preheat oven to 325 degrees. Line two cookie sheets with baking parchment; set aside. Fit a 16- or 18-inch pastry bag with a #6 plain round tube that has a $^1/_2$-inch opening. Fold down a deep cuff on the outside of the bag, and set the bag upright in a tall glass or jar; let stand.

In the large bowl of an electric mixer beat the butter with the vanilla, pepper, and salt until the butter is soft; add the sugar and beat until mixed. Add the eggs and additional white and beat to mix (it might look curdled but it is OK). Then, on low speed, add the flour, and finally the cornmeal, beating only until incorporated.

Remove the bowl from the mixer and stir in the lemon rind.

Transfer the dough to the pastry bag. Unfold the cuff and close the top of the bag by twisting it together. (The dough is quite stiff, and it will take some muscle to squeeze it out of the bag. Incidentally, it is always easier to work with a pastry bag at table height rather than counter height.)

Press out finger shapes of the dough about 4 inches long and 1 to 1½ inches apart (they spread out a bit during baking, like ladyfingers). When you reach the end of a strip, press the tip of the tube flat against the sheet to cut the dough away without leaving a tail, or just twist the bag and then lift it—whichever works best for you.

Bake two sheets at a time. At least once during baking reverse the sheets top to bottom and front to back to insure even browning. Bake for 25 to 30 minutes, until the cookies are golden and slightly darker around the edges. Do not underbake. Remove individually as they brown if they don't all brown at the same time.

With a wide metal spatula transfer to a brown paper bag or paper toweling.

If you bake one sheet alone, bake it in the middle of the oven. One sheet alone will bake in about 20 minutes.

Store in an airtight container.

Note: Any ground cornmeal seems to work well in these, but stoneground cornmeal is deliciously coarse and grainy. I especially like stoneground yellow cornmeal from The Vermont Country Store. You can order it by mail or phone. The mail order office is P.O. Box 3000, Manchester Center, VT 05255-3000; phone 802-362-2400.

Mucho-Macho Spice Bars

ABOUT 44 BARS

This is an Early American recipe for moist-yummy-chewy bars loaded with chopped raisins and a wonderful combination of tantalizing spices. (The original recipe didn't have all these spices.) In an unusual step, the raisins are chopped in a food processor.

The dough is formed into long, thin loaves, which are cut into bars after baking. It is best to use a flat-sided (only one raised rim) cookie sheet for baking these. If the cookie sheet has sides, use it upside down.

3 cups sifted unbleached flour
1 teaspoon baking soda
½ teaspoon salt
1½ teaspoons ground ginger
1 teaspoon ground cinnamon
½ teaspoon ground cloves
½ teaspoon dry powdered mustard
½ teaspoon finely ground black or white pepper (preferably freshly ground)
2 teaspoons powdered instant coffee
Optional—1½ ounces crystallized ginger (to make ¼ cup diced)
10 ounces (2 cups) raisins
1¼ cups granulated sugar
8 ounces (2 sticks) unsalted butter
2 tablespoons mild molasses ⎫
2 tablespoons honey ⎬ to equal ¼ cup
1 egg graded "large" ⎭

Adjust a rack to the middle of the oven and preheat oven to 350 degrees. Line two large cookie sheets with baking parchment or aluminum foil, shiny side up; set aside.

Sift together the flour, baking soda, salt, ginger, cinnamon, cloves, mustard, pepper, and coffee; set aside.

Cut the optional ginger into small dice and set aside.

Place the raisins in the bowl of a food processor fitted with the metal chopping blade. Add ¼ cup of the sugar (reserve remaining 1 cup sugar) and ¼ cup of the sifted dry ingredients (reserve remaining sifted ingredients).

Pulse the machine a few times and then process for 20 to 30 seconds, until the raisins are chopped into coarse pieces. Let stand.

In the large bowl of an electric mixer beat the butter until soft. Add the reserved 1 cup sugar and beat until mixed. Beat in the molasses, honey, and egg. Add the chopped raisins and diced ginger and beat until well mixed.

Now, on low speed, add half the reserved sifted dry ingredients and beat until incorporated.

Remove the bowl from the mixer. Add the remaining sifted dry ingredients and stir in by hand using a heavy wooden or rubber spatula.

Lightly flour a large cutting surface. Turn the dough out and, with floured hands, form it into a ball. Cut the ball in quarters. You are going to roll each piece of the dough with floured hands, rolling on the floured surface, until the piece is the length of your cookie sheets (mine are almost 17 inches long).

The dough will be soft; transfer it quickly, placing two of the rolls of dough lengthwise on each lined sheet.

They must be 4½ inches apart (or they will run into each other during baking), and they must be at least 1¾ inches away from the long sides of the cookie sheet (or they will run over). If the sheet isn't large enough for the lengths of dough to be at least that far apart, bake them only one loaf at a time.

Bake one sheet at a time for 22 to 23 minutes, reversing the sheet front to back once during baking to insure even baking. When they are done the loaves will have spread out quite wide. The tops will feel much too soft—feeling is not a test for these. Just time them carefully. Each baked loaf will be only a scant ½ inch thick and about 5 inches wide.

Remove the sheet from the oven and slide the parchment or foil off the sheet onto a large cutting board and, without waiting, use a long, heavy, sharp knife and cut each loaf crosswise into slices about 1¼ inches wide.

Bake and cut the slices on the second sheet.

Let the cut slices stand on the parchment or foil until they are firm enough to be transferred. Then, with a wide metal spatula, transfer the slices to a rack to finish cooling.

Even after they have cooled they will be (they should be) a bit soft. Therefore, it is best to store them two together, bottoms together, or they might lose their shapes.

You can either wrap these two together in clear cellophane, wax paper, or aluminum foil, or you can simply place them, lying flat, in an airtight box.

Bittersweet Chocolate Macaroons

ABOUT 20 MACAROONS

Dark, moist, and chewy, these have a divine texture. Although they are quite easy to make—and quick—they are elegant and classy and could be served at the most lavish event or at the simplest.

Chocolate macaroons are the number-one favorite of many people who are members of The-Chocolate-Lovers-of-the-World Association, of which I am chairperson of the board.

7 ounces (1⅓ cups) blanched (skinned) almonds
1 ounce semisweet chocolate
¾ cup granulated sugar
⅓ cup plus 2 tablespoons unsweetened cocoa powder (preferably Dutch process)
Pinch of salt
3 egg whites graded "large"

Adjust two racks to divide the oven into thirds and preheat oven to 350 degrees. Line two cookie sheets with baking parchment or with aluminum foil, shiny side up. Set aside.

Toast the almonds in a shallow pan in the oven for about 10 or 12 minutes, shaking the pan or stirring the nuts once or twice. Set aside to cool.

Remove 12 of the almonds. Place them on a board and with a long knife chop them into small pieces (to sprinkle on top of the macaroons before baking). Set aside.

Place the remaining almonds in the bowl of a food processor fitted with the metal chopping blade.

Chop the semisweet chocolate into small pieces and add it to the processor bowl. Add the sugar, cocoa, and salt.

Pulse the machine a few times and then process for about 30 seconds, until the almonds are fine.

With the motor running, add the egg whites through the feed tube and process until mixed.

To shape the mixture into round cookies, either use a pastry bag (the bag should be about 12 inches long or longer) fitted with a ½-inch (#6) plain round tube, or you can drop them from a teaspoon. Use one spoon to pick up the mixture, another to push it off. Use a well-rounded teaspoonful for each macaroon. The rounds should be placed about 1 inch apart.

Sprinkle the tops with the chopped nuts.

Bake for 10 minutes, reversing the sheets top to bottom and front to back once during baking. When done, the macaroons should feel soft but dry, not sticky.

Definitely do not overbake.

With a firm metal spatula transfer the macaroons to a rack to cool.

Store in an airtight container or loosely covered—they do well either way. But I think these are best when very fresh.

Grammie Raichlen's Ribbon Cookies

ABOUT 40 COOKIES,
EACH ABOUT 4 INCHES
LONG

Crisp, thin, delicate, delicious, and elegant. Fragile! They're quick and easy to make, but you need a cookie press with a flat ribbon tip. I just bought a new one in a hardware store. It's made by Mirro, and it's great fun. (If you don't have one, you don't know what you're missing.)

Steven Raichlen, who has written many wonderful, award-winning cookbooks, is a good friend and neighbor. He probably inherited much of his cooking talent from his grandmother. She's a fabulous cook, famous for her cookies. Especially these, which she has been making since she was married sixty-seven years ago.

8 ounces (2 sticks) unsalted butter
1 teaspoon vanilla extract
½ teaspoon salt
½ cup granulated sugar
1 egg graded "large"
2½ cups sifted unbleached flour

Adjust a rack to the center of the oven (it is best to bake these one sheet at a time) and preheat oven to 375 degrees. Line cookie sheets with baking parchment or aluminum foil, shiny side up, or you can bake these on unlined sheets.

In the large bowl of an electric mixer beat the butter, vanilla, salt, and sugar until thoroughly mixed. Beat in the egg. Then, on low speed, gradually beat in the flour.

Fill the cookie press, packing the dough compactly in order to avoid air holes.

Hold the cookie press in a semi-horizontal position to the sheet. Check to make sure that the ridged side of the ribbon faces up. Form a ribbon of the dough the length of the sheet. The ribbon of dough should lie flat, but if it is wavy in places, it's OK. When you reach the end of the sheet, make a few reverse turns of the handle of the cookie press, which will cut off the dough. Repeat, forming four ribbons on each sheet.

Bake for about 9 minutes, until the ribbons are lightly colored on the edges. Reverse the sheet front to back once during baking to insure even browning.

Watch them carefully. They can suddenly become too dark. How do I know? Three guesses.

As soon as you remove the sheet from the oven, use a long, sharp knife, and cut across all the ribbons at once, cutting them into fourths. (If they cool before you cut them, they will crumble.) And, immediately, with a wide metal spatula, transfer to a rack or to a brown paper bag to cool.

Handle with care. Store in an airtight container.

Baguettes

16 TO 18 COOKIES

This is an old French recipe for cookies that are shaped like extra-long lady fingers. (The ingredients are similar to lady fingers, but with fewer eggs.) They are hard, dry, and plain, not rich. They're simple, but also elegant and classy, delicious with tea and coffee, or even with wine. They keep well, they last well, and if you like to use a pastry bag, these are a breeze to make.

⅓ cup unblanched almonds
Scant ½ cup granulated sugar
Pinch of salt
1 egg plus 1 yolk graded "large"
½ teaspoon vanilla extract
1 cup plus 3 tablespoons sifted unbleached flour

Adjust two racks to divide the oven into thirds and preheat oven to 350 degrees. Butter and flour two cookie sheets (shake off excess flour). Set aside.

Fit a 12- or 16-inch pastry bag with a #6 plain round tube that has a ½-inch opening. Fold down a deep cuff on the outside of the bag. Twist the tube end and then push it up into the bag a bit to prevent leakage. Set the bag upright in a tall glass or jar; let stand.

First toast the almonds. Place them in a shallow pan in the oven for about 10 minutes, shaking the pan a few times, until you can smell toasted almonds when you open the oven door. Set aside to cool. Then, on a chopping surface, with a long and sharp knife, chop the nuts medium-fine (some will be powdery, some coarse); set aside.

Place the sugar, salt, egg, and yolk in the small bowl of an electric mixer and beat at high speed for 3 to 4 minutes, until the mixture has whitened and forms a ribbon when the beaters are raised. Add the vanilla and flour and beat briefly on low speed only until mixed.

Transfer the mixture to the pastry bag. Shape and bake now, without waiting.

Unfold the cuff. Untwist the pastry bag to open the tube end. Form shapes like your little finger but longer (5 to 6 inches long). At the end of each strip, to remove the tube without leaving a tail, either cut the batter away with a small knife or press the tube down flat against the sheet to cut the batter. Shape the cookies about an inch apart.

Sprinkle the cookies generously with the chopped almonds, and then, with a fingertip, press on the almonds very gently to keep them from falling off.

Bake two sheets at a time for 13 to 15 minutes, reversing the sheets top to bottom and front to back once during baking. Bake until the cookies are only slightly colored (they will remain quite pale).

With a wide metal spatula transfer the cookies to a rack to cool. Store in an airtight container.

Chocolate O's

These cookies are individually shaped by hand into charming "O" shapes. I recently threaded a black velvet ribbon through a few of them and wore it as a necklace. Everyone admired my jewelry. When I said that they were cookies, my friends ate them right off me. And loved them.

30 TO 35 COOKIES

3 ounces unsweetened chocolate
2 cups sifted unbleached flour
$\frac{1}{2}$ teaspoon baking powder
$\frac{1}{4}$ teaspoon salt
4 ounces (1 stick) unsalted butter
1 teaspoon vanilla extract
$\frac{1}{2}$ cup granulated sugar
2 tablespoons dark rum or whiskey
1 egg graded "large"
Optional—milk (to use as topping)
Optional—Crystal sugar (to use as topping—see page 5)

Adjust two racks to divide the oven into thirds and preheat oven to 350 degrees. Line cookie sheets with baking parchment or aluminum foil, shiny side up; set aside.

Place the chocolate in the top part of a small double boiler over warm water on moderate heat. Let stand until melted. Remove from the hot water; set aside.

Sift together the flour, baking powder, and salt; set aside.

In the large bowl of an electric mixer beat the butter until soft. Beat in the vanilla and sugar, then the rum or whiskey, the egg, and the chocolate. Beat until mixed. Add the sifted dry ingredients and beat on low speed only until incorporated.

Refrigerate the dough for 20 to 30 minutes.

Each cookie will be formed from a piece of the dough about the size of a small walnut. First shape one as a sample. Work a piece of dough a bit in your hand, and between your hands roll it into an oval shape.

It is best to work on a wood surface. Lightly flour the surface. Roll the dough back and forth gently under both hands—with your fingers spread—to form a shape 6 or 7 inches long and about ½ inch wide in the middle with tapered ends.

This dough is very tender; handle it gently.

Place the cookie on the lined sheet, and, as you do so, curve it into an "O" with the two ends crossing about ½ inch before the ends (in other words, the ends should extend ½ inch beyond where they cross each other).

With a teaspoon divide the dough into 30 to 34 pieces and place them any which way next to your work space. Cover them loosely with plastic wrap. Then continue to shape all of the pieces and place them on the lined sheets about one inch apart.

Brush the optional milk on a few of the cookies at a time, and then sprinkle them with a bit of the optional crystal sugar. Continue to brush and sugar all of the cookies.

Bake two sheets at a time, reversing the sheets top to bottom and front to back once during baking. Bake for 15 minutes.

With a metal spatula transfer the cookies to racks to cool.

Store in an airtight container.

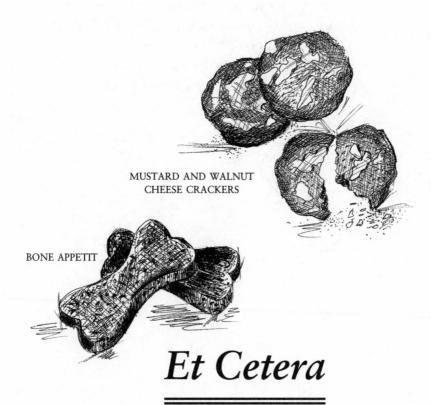

MUSTARD AND WALNUT
CHEESE CRACKERS

BONE APPETIT

Et Cetera

BONE APPÉTIT
SKINNY BREADSTICKS
PARCHMENT CRACKERS
MUSTARD AND WALNUT CHEESE CRACKERS
ENGLISH PEPPER CRACKERS
GRANITA'S POTS DE CRÈME AU CHOCOLAT
CAMPANILE'S PANNA COTTA

Bone Appétit

12 TO 18 DOG BISCUITS

These are gourmet dog biscuits.

Bonkers was a special dog who belonged to my brother and sister-in-law, Basil and Connie Heatter. Bonkers was the boss and he knew it. He lived to be nineteen years old. Connie regularly made these dog biscuits for him, and I don't know if they contributed to his remarkable age, but I do know that he adored them and could never get enough.

Although Connie cut them with a heart-shaped cookie cutter—to express her sentiments—you can buy cutters shaped like dog biscuits, in different sizes, in most kitchen shops (Williams Sonoma has them), or you can cut them into bars with a knife.

Incidentally, I've been told that the nutritional yeast in these will repel fleas (but the dog must eat it, not have it rubbed over his body). The other ingredients will, of course, make your dog healthy and happy and the smartest and strongest dog on the block.

All of the following dry ingredients are available in health food stores.

1/4 cup unprocessed bran
1 cup unsifted whole wheat flour
1/4 cup raw wheat germ
1 tablespoon powdered bone meal
1 tablespoon nutritional yeast
1/4 cup dry powdered milk
2 egg whites
One 6-ounce jar (about 2/3 cup) chicken or beef and vegetable baby food

Adjust a rack to the middle of the oven and preheat oven to 300 degrees.

Place all the ingredients in a large bowl and stir—and stir—until completely mixed.

Flour a pastry cloth and a rolling pin.

Form the dough into a mound and roll it out on the pastry cloth with the rolling pin until it is about ⅓ inch thick. Cut with cookie cutters (see above introduction). Or with a long, sharp knife, trim the edges and then cut the dough into slices about 1¼ inches wide. Then cut the slices into 3-inch lengths. Place the biscuits on a cookie sheet; they can be close to each other.

Bake for 1 hour, reversing the sheet front to back once during baking, and turn the biscuits upside down once during baking.

After 1 hour, turn off the oven but let the biscuits cool in the oven for about ½ hour, then remove from the oven and let stand until cool.

Bowwow!

Note: If you are making these for a small dog, I would think that the dough should be rolled thinner, in which case they don't have to bake as long.

P.S. I don't have a dog. After I wrote this recipe I gave samples of the biscuits to all my friends who have or know some dogs. During the next few days everyone except a certain gentleman friend called to tell me how much the dogs enjoyed them . . . the dogs barked and ran around looking for more.

Finally, I called the gentleman and asked, "What about the dog biscuits?" He answered, "Oh, I just ate them today. I love them. They're wonderful."

"But they were dog biscuits—they were for a dog."

"But I got hungry, and they were delicious."

Skinny Breadsticks

ABOUT 50 TO 70
16-INCH BREADSTICKS

This is a yeast dough. It is Wolfgang Puck's recipe for his world-famous pizzas. The breadsticks are as thin as a pencil. They are fun to make, and show-stopper gorgeous to serve standing up in a tall glass. They are very fragile, so handle with care. Of course these are great with any meal, but they are also a big hit served with drinks.

You will need a pizza wheel (a round blade on a handle), a ruler, and a thermometer to test the warm water.

To make the full amount of breadsticks plan to spend at least two hours in the kitchen, but, if you wish, you can use some of the dough to make delicious small dinner rolls or a pizza or two. (Wolf makes four individual pizzas from the whole recipe.)

These breadsticks will last, and last, a long time.

1 envelope active dry yeast
¼ cup warm water (105 to 115 degrees)
1 teaspoon salt
¾ cup plus 2 tablespoons cold water
2 tablespoons olive oil (see Notes)
1 tablespoon honey
3 cups unsifted bread flour
Optional—about ½ cup sesame seeds
1 egg (size doesn't matter)
Coarse salt
Optional—coarse or fine black or white pepper
Optional—dried green peppercorns
Optional—powdered dried onion and/or garlic
Optional—minced dried shallots
Optional—poppy seeds or caraway seeds

Add the yeast to the warm water, stir with a knife, and let stand 10 minutes.

In a measuring cup, add the salt to the cold water and stir to dissolve. Add the oil and honey and mix well. Set aside.

Place the flour in the bowl of a food processor fitted with the metal chopping blade. With the motor running, add the yeast mixture through the feed tube. Then stir the cold water with the salt, oil, and honey again and pour it back and forth from one cup to the other to clean the two cups (the honey will settle; be sure to get it all); with the motor running, add it through the feed tube. Process 45 seconds.

Turn out onto a lightly floured surface and knead briefly only until smooth.

You need a bowl with a 6- to 8-cup capacity (or larger). Spread the inside of the bowl with olive oil. Place the dough in the bowl and turn the dough upside down in order to oil it all over. Cover the bowl with plastic wrap and let stand for about 45 minutes, until the dough is almost double in volume.

Because I live in Florida where it is usually warm, I let yeast dough rise in the mailbox. In cooler temperatures, let the dough rise in the oven with the oven light on.

Meanwhile, place the optional sesame seeds in a wide frying pan over moderate heat. Shake the pan and/or stir the seeds for about 5 minutes until golden; set aside.

Using the largest cookie sheets you have, cut baking parchment or aluminum foil to fit them.

Lightly flour a large cutting board and a rolling pin. Turn the dough out onto the board. With the palms of your hands, flatten the dough well. Fold the dough in half and flatten it again. Then, with the floured rolling pin, roll the dough into a rectangle about 10 by 18 inches. Let stand about 10 minutes. Then continue to roll until the dough is only ⅛ inch thick and about 12 or 13 inches by 18 to 20 inches.

Flour the surface under the dough lightly and also flour the top of the dough lightly (to prevent a ruler from sticking to it). The best way to cut the bread sticks is with a pizza wheel, cutting against a ruler. Trim one short end to make it straight. Then place the ruler on top of the dough, ¼ inch away from the trimmed edge, and cut the first strip. Move the ruler ¼ inch away and cut again. Repeat a few times. After cutting a few strips, place them on a lined cookie sheet. The 12- or 13-inch lengths will stretch out to about 16 inches (or as long as your cookie sheets) when you transfer them from the board to the sheet.

When you place them on the sheet, you can make them either straight or wiggly. Place the strips the long way about ½ inch apart.

Beat the egg just to mix. Brush it on about half of the breadsticks on one sheet.

You can either leave them as they are or sprinkle them with a bit of coarse salt or you can use a combination of the salt and some of the optional sesame seeds, pepper, onion and/or garlic powder, dried shallots, and/or additional seeds. I like the bread sticks best with just a bit of coarse salt, black pepper, and green peppercorns (see Notes).

Brush and sprinkle the remaining breadsticks about half a sheet at a time.

Let the breadsticks stand for about 20 minutes (it doesn't hurt them if they stand a little longer).

Meanwhile, adjust two racks to divide the oven into thirds and pre-heat oven to 400 degrees.

Place two sheets in the oven to bake. Reverse the sheets top to bottom and front to back a few times during baking to insure even browning. They should bake about 15 to 18 minutes or less, depending on their thickness, until golden brown (never darker) all over. If some of the breadsticks are done before others, they can be removed individually when ready. When they are all done, you can slide the parchment or foil off the sheets and slide the sheets under additional pieces of parchment or foil (even if the sheets are hot) with bread-sticks on them that are ready to be baked.

The baked breadsticks can cool on the parchment or foil. They will become crisp as they cool.

When cool, store in an airtight container. If you don't have an airtight container that is long enough, wrap them all carefully in long pieces of plastic wrap and/or aluminum foil.

If, after awhile, they lose their crispness, reheat and then cool before serving.

Notes: If you have one of the great new flavored olive oils (chili, garlic, herbs, or some combination) use 1 tablespoon of the flavored oil and 1 tablespoon of unflavored oil. I use a really hot chili fajita oil (from the Santa Barbara Olive Company in Santa Ynez, California. Phone 800-624-4896).

I mix the topping ingredients ahead of time on a piece of paper or in a shallow dish. I use equal parts of coarse sea salt, freshly ground black pepper, and dried green peppercorns ground with a mortar and pestle. This is a hot combination; use with caution.

Variation

Parchment Crackers. If you wrap some of the above dough (I guess this would work with any similar yeast dough) and refrigerate it for several hours or overnight you will be able to roll it as thin as parchment paper. While rolling out the dough, stop occasionally and let the dough rest for several minutes, and then continue to roll. When the dough is thin enough, trim the edges with a pizza wheel and then cut the dough into pieces about 3 by 5 inches. Pierce the dough in several places with a fork. With a wide metal spatula transfer the crackers to unlined, unbuttered cookie sheets. Bake in a 400-degree oven. If you bake two sheets at a time, reverse the sheets top to bottom and front to back a few times during baking to insure even baking. If you bake one sheet alone reverse it front to back a few times. When the crackers barely begin to color use a metal spatula and turn the crackers upside down. Bake only until the crackers are a light golden color. Do not overbake. When done, the crackers will be pale in some areas and honey colored in spots. (Of course they should bake until completely crisp, but the flavor is best if they are barely colored.) Cool and then store in an airtight container.

Mustard and Walnut Cheese Crackers

These are crisp cheese and walnut crackers with a wonderful hot-spicy flavor. Serve them with drinks or at the table with soup or salad.

This recipe uses the same technique as icebox cookies. The dough must be shaped into a roll and refrigerated for several hours or overnight (or longer if you wish) before it is sliced and baked.

ABOUT 48 CRACKERS

4 ounces (1 stick) unsalted butter
1 cup sifted unbleached flour
½ teaspoon baking powder
½ teaspoon black or white pepper ground fine (preferably freshly ground)
½ teaspoon dry mustard powder
¼ teaspoon ground cayenne
½ pound sharp cheddar cheese
1 tablespoon prepared mustard
¼ teaspoon Tabasco sauce
6 ounces (generous 1½ cups) walnut halves or large pieces

Cut the butter into slices about ½ inch wide; let stand at room temperature (it should be at room temperature when you use it).

Sift together the flour, baking powder, pepper, mustard powder, and cayenne; set aside.

Cut the cheddar cheese into medium-small pieces and place in the bowl of a food processor fitted with the metal chopping blade. Process about 20 seconds. Add the sifted dry ingredients and pulse the machine 7 or 8 times to mix.

Add the butter and the prepared mustard and process, adding the Tabasco sauce through the feed tube. When the ingredients are well mixed, scrape into a bowl. The mixture might be uneven and might need to be stirred a bit. It will be thick and sticky.

Add the walnuts. Stir them in until evenly mixed into the dough.

Lightly flour a work surface. Place the mixture by large spoonfuls in a strip about 12 to 13 inches long on the floured surface. Flour your hands and shape the dough into an even and smooth roll 12 to 13 inches long and 1½ to 2 inches in diameter with flat ends.

With a pastry brush remove excess flour from the roll, then wrap it in plastic wrap.

Refrigerate for several hours or overnight (or longer).

When you are ready to bake adjust two racks to divide the oven into thirds (if you are going to bake only one sheet at a time adjust a rack in the center of the oven). Preheat oven to 350 degrees.

Unwrap the dough and place it on a cutting board. Using a very sharp knife, cut slices ¼ inch wide and place them 1 to 1½ inches apart on unlined and unbuttered cookie sheets.

Bake for 12 to 15 minutes (or a bit longer if necessary), until the crackers are lightly colored. Once or twice during baking reverse the sheets top to bottom and front to back (if you are baking one sheet alone turn it front to back during baking).

Spread out a large brown paper bag or several pieces of paper toweling to place the baked crackers on.

The crackers should be removed from the cookie sheets as soon as they are ready; some will probably be done before others. With a wide metal spatula remove each cracker as soon as it is done. Do not overbake. Place the crackers on the paper bag or paper toweling and let stand until cool.

Store in an airtight container.

Note: Since these are rather fragile, when I make them to give as a gift I place them in a glass jar.

English Pepper Crackers

24 3½-INCH WAFERS

Perfectly plain crackers, these are good served with cheese and wine, or with soup or salad at the table. The crackers are paper-thin, and easy to make (if you like rolling dough with a rolling pin). Before I started making these I always bought English water crackers; now I make these. These are more tender and more flavorful.

One afternoon recently a famous French chef named Guy LeRoy came to visit me. I served these crackers, French brie, and Grgich Hills Chardonnay. I can't tell you how much he (we) ate and drank. He asked for the recipe for the crackers, and he raved about them. You will too.

3 tablespoons unsalted butter
1½ cups sifted unbleached flour
1 teaspoon baking powder
1 teaspoon finely ground and freshly ground white pepper
½ teaspoon salt
4 tablespoons ice water

Adjust two racks to divide the oven into thirds and preheat oven to 350 degrees. You can use unbuttered and unlined cookie sheets or you can line the sheets with baking parchment.

Cut the butter the long way into quarters, then cut through all four quarters together, cutting ¼-inch slices. Refrigerate.

Place the flour, baking powder, pepper, and salt in the bowl of a food processor fitted with the metal chopping blade. Pulse once or twice to mix. Add the butter, pulse a few times, and then process for only 4 or 5 seconds, until the mixture resembles coarse meal. With the motor running, add the water through the feed tube and let the machine run for about 8 to 10 seconds, until the ingredients just barely begin to hold together. The mixture should look like coarse crumbs.

Turn the dough out onto a length of plastic wrap. Fold the plastic over the dough, press against the plastic to form the dough into a compact ball, then unwrap the dough and cut in half. Work with half at a time.

Lightly flour a pastry cloth and a rolling pin. Roll out the dough until it is very, very thin (⅟₁₆ inch or less). You may turn the dough upside down a few times while rolling, and reflour the cloth and rolling pin as necessary.

With a four-pronged table fork, prick holes about ½ inch apart all over the dough.

Traditionally these are cut with a plain, round 3½-inch cookie cutter, but you can use any size and any shape cutter, or you can cut the dough into squares or rectangles with a pizza wheel or a knife.

Before you squeeze all the scraps together, see if there are any pieces large enough to cut small squares, rectangles, triangles, or crescents. (Cut the crescents with the same round cutter.) Reserve any scraps that are too small to cut.

Place the crackers on the cookie sheets. They can be placed right next to each other, as they shrink a bit during baking.

Roll and cut the second half of the dough. Any small scraps can be pressed together, rolled, and cut.

Bake for 15 to 18 minutes, reversing the sheets top to bottom and front to back once during baking to insure even baking. These should bake until they are absolutely dry and crisp and only barely colored (a pale golden tint).

Cool (they can cool right on the cookie sheets) and then store in an airtight container.

Granita's Pots de Crème au Chocolat

6 PORTIONS

Pots de crème is the king of custards, and Granita is a spectacular restaurant in Malibu, California, that belongs to my friends Barbara Lazaroff and her husband, Wolfgang Puck. This is probably the most popular dessert they serve (the regular customers call ahead to reserve it because it sells out early).

At Granita they put each dish of pots de crème on a wide, flat plate and surround it with a few of Barbara's chocolate biscotti (see page 17) and a variety of fresh berries. The top is left beautifully bare. It is gorgeous and delicious and elegant, yet it is not difficult to make.

The only thing that could go wrong with this would happen if you baked it at too high a temperature. Correctly made, it is tender and delicate and as smooth as satin, but if the oven is too hot the custard will develop bubbles and it will be uneven, watery, tough, and unpleasant. To be positive that this will not happen, I bake it at an extra-low temperature—the result is magical. The baked and cooled custards should be refrigerated for at least 3 hours, or all day if you wish. But Jason Epstein, my editor (and chef extraordinaire), makes them a day ahead and refrigerates them overnight; he raves about them.

You will need individual custard cups. The straight-sided, white pottery cups (individual soufflé dishes) made by Apilco in France are my favorites. They are generally available in kitchen shops. You want the ones that are 3½ inches wide, 1½ inches high, and have a ½-cup capacity (not filled all the way to the top). You could also use Pyrex cups; they will work fine—they just won't look as good.

I have made these with Valrhona chocolate (made in France) and with Lindt "excellence" (made in Switzerland). Both are equally delicious.

4 ounces semisweet chocolate
½ cup milk

2 *cups heavy cream*
½ *cup granulated sugar*
½ *vanilla bean, split the long way*
5 *yolks from eggs graded "large"*

Adjust a rack to the center of the oven and preheat oven to 275 degrees. Arrange six custard cups in a shallow pan; the pan should be no deeper than the cups. (If the pan is aluminum, sprinkle about ½ teaspoon cream of tartar in the pan—it will prevent the pan from discoloring.)

Break or cut the chocolate into small pieces.

Place the milk, cream, ¼ cup of the sugar (reserve remaining ¼ cup sugar), the vanilla bean, and the chocolate in a saucepan over medium heat. Stir occasionally until the mixture comes to a boil.

Meanwhile, place the yolks and remaining ¼ cup sugar in a large mixing bowl, and stir/whisk a bit to mix (do not beat enough to make foam or bubbles).

When the milk mixture comes to a boil, adjust the heat, stir, and let boil for 1 minute. Then, gradually, pour the boiling hot mixture over the yolks, and stir/whisk to mix (again, do not make foam or bubbles).

Strain the mixture through a strainer into a container with a spout. With a spoon or a knife scrape the seeds of the vanilla bean into the hot mixture and discard the bean.

Pour the custard into the cups, leaving a bit of headroom in each cup.

Place the pan with the filled cups in the oven. Pour hot water into the pan halfway up the sides of the cups. Cover the cups with a cookie sheet or a large piece of aluminum foil.

Bake for 45 minutes. (These are best when baked only until not quite done. They continue to firm up while they cool and chill. The usual test—"insert a small sharp knife; when it comes out clean, the custard is done"—does not work for these. By the time the knife comes out clean, these are overdone. The only way I know to tell when these are done is by the clock . . . if your oven temperature is correct.)

Remove the cookie sheet or foil from the top of the cups. Carefully remove the pan from the oven. Let stand for about 20 minutes, until you can touch the cups. Remove them from the water, dry them, and let stand, uncovered, until cooled to room temperature.

Refrigerate, uncovered, for about 3 hours, or all day if you wish. Serve directly from the refrigerator. The colder they are, the better.

Campanile's Panna Cotta

8 PORTIONS

A divine, individually molded dessert. It just barely holds its shape. It quivers. It shivers. It trembles deliciously.

Panna cotta is Italian for "cooked cream." This recipe is from my friend Nancy Silverton. Nancy serves this panna cotta at Campanile, the popular restaurant she and her husband, Mark Peel, own in Los Angeles. (Incidentally, the building that houses Campanile used to be Charlie Chaplin's headquarters.)

Nancy says that you should make this early in the day for that evening. By the following day it loses its wiggle—it becomes more firm. But I think it is still very special and wonderful even the following day.

Make it in individual ramekins. I use individual soufflé dishes (the same as those used in the previous recipe). You could also use Pyrex custard cups. The dishes or cups should have a 4- or 5-ounce capacity.

3 tablespoons cold water
1 envelope unflavored gelatin
3 cups heavy cream
1 cup milk
¼ cup granulated sugar
Pinch of salt
1 vanilla bean

Measure the water into a small cup and sprinkle the gelatin on top. Let stand.

Place the cream, milk, sugar, and salt in a large, heavy saucepan (preferably one with at least a 4-quart capacity). Slit the vanilla bean lengthwise, scrape out the seeds, and add the seeds and bean to the cream mixture. Place over high heat and stir frequently until the mixture comes to a boil. (Do not walk away—it might boil over. If it starts to boil up high, raise the pan from the heat, and lower the heat as necessary.) Let boil 1 minute.

Remove from the heat, add the soaked gelatin, and stir to dissolve. Strain through a wide strainer set over a bowl.

Lightly oil the insides of eight 4- to 5-ounce individual soufflé dishes or Pyrex custard cups and place them on a tray that will fit in the refrigerator.

Ladle or pour the panna cotta into the dishes, leaving a bit of head-room on each.

Let stand to cool, then place in the refrigerator for a minimum of 3 hours.

RASPBERRY-STRAWBERRY SAUCE
(Make this early in the day for that evening.)
¼ cup plus 2 tablespoons granulated sugar
¼ cup water
¼ cup strawberry or raspberry preserves
*12 ounces (3 cups) frozen raspberries (individually frozen with no
      sugar)*
Two 1-pint boxes fresh strawberries
3 tablespoons Framboise or cognac

Place the sugar, water, and preserves in a saucepan over high heat. Stir until the mixture comes to a boil. Add the raspberries (which may or may not still be frozen), stir briefly, boil, covered, for 1½ minutes, then remove the cover and boil, uncovered, for 1½ minutes.

Strain through a fine but wide strainer set over a large bowl. Rub the mixture through the strainer and discard the seeds. Let cool.

Meanwhile, prepare the strawberries. Wash them quickly in a large bowl of cold water. Remove the hulls, and place on toweling to drain. Then cut the berries into quarters. Stir the strawberries and Framboise or cognac into the raspberry mixture; refrigerate.

Unmold the desserts just before serving. First cut around the sides of one dish with a small, sharp knife. Then place the dish in a bowl of very hot, shallow water; let stand 15 seconds. Dry the dish, cover with a flat dessert plate, and invert. Lift off and remove the dish. Continue to unmold the desserts one by one.

Spoon a generous amount of the sauce alongside each panna cotta.

Note: Some time try this sensational sauce with vanilla ice cream or with raspberry, strawberry, or vanilla yogurt. Or just with a spoon.

Index

Spice cookies (*cont'd*)
mucho-macho bars, 209–11
peanut raisin, 146–47
pepper and ginger wafers, 132–33
pfeffernüsse, 179–81
rum and pepper gingersnaps, 176–78
Swedish, 171–73
Strawberry-raspberry sauce, 237–38
Sugar:
brown. *See* Brown sugar
crystal, 5–6
vanilla, turbinado style, 6
Suki, Chef, 107
Swedish spice cookies, 171–73
Sweet and hot meringues, 125–26
Sweet Celebrations, 5
Sweet pretzels, 204–6

Taylor oven thermometers, 9
Tea cakes, brown sugar, 192–93
Thermometers, oven, 9–10
Timing, 12
Toll House recipe, 151, 152
$250.00 cookie recipe, 148–50

Vanilla:
bean and lemon zwieback, 42–44
sugar, turbinado style, 6
Vermont Country Store, 208
Villa D'Este (Lake Como, Italy), 34–36

Wafers:
French honey, 185–86
Moravian, 163–64
oatmeal, 95–96
pepper and ginger, 132–33

skinny maple pecan, 93–94
skinny peanut, 89–90
skinny walnut, 91–92
Wakefield, Ruth, 152
Walnut(s):
black, pearls, 144–45
chocolate chip sour cream cookies, 99–100
and coconut oatmeal bars, 69–70
heirloom icebox cookies, 158–59
horns (a.k.a. rugelach), 194–96
jumbles, 113–14
Key Largo oatmeal cookies, 129–31
kisses, Hungarian, 123–24
Martha's Vineyard hermits, 112
and mustard cheese crackers, 229–30
Palm Beach brownies with chocolate-covered mints, 79–82
passion, 50
positively-the-absolutely-best-chocolate-chip cookies, 151–52
Saturday night meringues, 121–22
and sour cherry chocolate hermits, 101–2
$250.00 cookie recipe, 148–50
wafers, skinny, 91–92
Wax paper, 4
Whole wheat flour, in multigrain and seed biscotti, 28–30
Wolff, Renée, 150
Wrapping cookies individually, 4

Zwieback, 15
vanilla bean and lemon, 42–44
see also Biscotti

ABOUT THE AUTHOR

MAIDA HEATTER is the author of seven dessert books. Two of her previous books—*Maida Heatter's Book of Great Cookies* and the *New York Times* bestseller *Maida Heatter's Book of Great Chocolate Desserts*—were awarded the James Beard Book Award. She is the daughter of Gabriel Heatter, the radio commentator. She studied fashion illustration at Pratt Institute and has done fashion illustrating and designing, made jewelry, and painted. But her first love has always been cooking. She taught it in classes in her home, in department stores, and at cooking schools across the country. For many years she made all the desserts for a popular Miami Beach restaurant owned by her late husband, Ralph Daniels.

She prepared desserts for the 1983 Summit of Industrialized Nations at Colonial Williamsburg, Virginia, for President Reagan and six other heads of state.

Ms. Heatter's late daughter, Toni Evins, a painter and illustrator, did the drawings for the first six of Ms. Heatter's books.

ABOUT THE TYPE

This book was set in Sabon, a typeface designed by the well-known German typographer Jan Tschichold (1902–74). Sabon's design is based on the original letterforms of Claude Garamond and was created specifically to be used for three sources: foundry type for hand composition, Linotype, and Monotype. Tschichold named his typeface for the famous Frankfurt typefounder Jacques Sabon, who died in 1580.